Heroes of the Home Run

 A TARGET BOOK

Heroes
of the
Home
Run

Edited, with commentary by Bennett Wayne

GARRARD PUBLISHING COMPANY
CHAMPAIGN, ILLINOIS

Library of Congress Cataloging in Publication Data

Wayne, Bennett.
      Heroes of the home run.

      (A Target book)
      SUMMARY: Brief biographies of ten major league
baseball stars well known for their outstanding batting
records.

      1. Baseball—Biography. [1. Baseball—Biography]
I. Title.
GV865.A1W35   796.357′092′2 [B] [920]   73–6750
ISBN 0–8116–4903–2

Picture credits:

Brown Brothers: pp. 6, 13, 16, 18, 33 (both), 41, 59, 62 (both),
      86, 90, 119 (both), 129 (bottom), 132
Culver Pictures, Inc.: pp. 26, 43, 44, 52, 64, 150
Photoworld: p. 36
United Press International: pp. 8, 48, 68, 76, 83, 92, 93, 96, 98,
      103, 111, 114, 138, 143, 160, cover
Wide World Photos: pp. 123, 126, 129 (top), 147, 157

Contents

The Fence-Busters

Here are the hitters, the sluggers, the heroes of the home run! Every one of these men had a lifetime batting average of .325 or more. Every one of them has been elected to baseball's Hall of Fame.

The great teams of the past included talented pitchers and catchers, outstanding base runners and fielders. But it was the man with the bat who most appealed to the fans. It was the smack of wood on horsehide and the sight of the ball sailing out of the park that brought them to their feet.

Newspaper stories gave every detail in the lives of the famous batters. Little boys tagged after them. Admirers begged for their autographs. They were called iron man, sultan, rajah— king! The fans adored them.

There was clumsy-looking Ol' Honus Wagner, who hit .300 or better for seventeen years; hot-tempered Ty Cobb, whose brilliant record as hitter, fielder, and base runner has never been surpassed; Nap Lajoie, thought to be the greatest of all natural hitters; Tris Speaker, whose lifetime average of .344 stands high in the record books; hardworking Rogers Hornsby, who batted .400 or more for three years; the immortal Babe Ruth, greatest slugger of them all; Lou Gehrig, the "pride of the Yankees"; Joe DiMaggio, whose 56-game hitting streak will never be forgotten; Ted Williams, who piled up an amazing batting record in spite of two hitches in the Marine Corps.

The life stories of these home-run heroes—their early days on the diamond, their most exciting games, and the great men of baseball who were their teammates and opponents—crowd the pages of this book. These stories can be read partly as a history of baseball, partly as a history of America. But mostly they should be read just for fun!

Honus Wagner
The Flying Dutchman

by Sam and Beryl Epstein

When awkward-looking Ol' Honus scooped
up a grounder in his huge hands, he was
likely to gather up some pebbles too!
Even so, he was the greatest shortstop in
baseball history—and one of the game's
mighty sluggers.

9

Honus Wagner
The Flying Dutchman

It was a cold February afternoon in the year 1896. Several young men stood beside the railroad tracks in a little Pennsylvania town. One was John Peter Wagner. His friends called him Honus, or Hans.

"It's your turn, Honus," somebody said.

Honus picked up a stone in his huge right hand. His arm moved back and then snapped forward. The stone flew through the air.

"Look at that!" a friend said. "What's the use of having a pitching contest with him? Honus throws twice as far as the rest of us, without even trying!"

A stranger came along the tracks. "I'm looking for a Honus Wagner," he said.

"That's me," Honus said.

The stranger looked at the tall, awkward young man. Honus was bowlegged. His arms were so long that his hands seemed to touch his knees. His clothes were shabby. He had stuck a chicken feather in his derby hat. He looked like a clown.

The stranger laughed. Honus didn't mind. He just grinned.

"A man in Pittsburgh told me you play ball," the stranger said.

"Sometimes," Honus said. "I used to play on Sundays with my brothers. The rest of the week we all worked in the coal mines."

He picked up a stone as he spoke, and let it fly down the tracks. The stranger could hardly believe his eyes when he saw how far it went.

"Honus isn't telling you the whole story," another young man said. "The Wagner brothers had their own team. It beat all the other teams around here. Al, Honus's brother, is a real professional ballplayer now. He got Honus a job with an Ohio team last summer."

"What position did you play?" the stranger asked.

Honus looked surprised. "All positions," he said. "I even pitched once in a while."

"What do you do now?" the stranger asked.

"Oh, odd jobs," Honus said. He threw another stone.

Again the stranger watched it fly down the tracks. "My name is Ed Barrow," he said. "I'm signing up players for my team in Paterson, New Jersey. I'm paying the rest of the team $100 a month. But I'll pay you $125. How about it?"

Honus grinned. "That's a lot of money!" he said. "Sure, Mr. Barrow. I'll play for you."

Years later, when Barrow was managing the Yankees, he often told how he had discovered the great Honus Wagner.

"Wagner is the greatest all-round ballplayer of all time," Barrow always said. Many experts agreed with him.

Wagner became the star of the minor-league Paterson team almost overnight. The fans loved him because he was so good natured. They loved him because he helped the team win games too. He could play well in any position.

"He walks like a crab, fields like an octopus, and hits like the devil!" one sportswriter said.

There was only one major league in those days —the National League. Scouts from almost every National League team came to Paterson to watch the big 22-year-old rookie. Several wanted to buy his contract. Barrow knew Honus was too good to stay in Paterson very long. He sold Honus to Louisville in 1897.

The Louisville manager, Fred Clarke, put Honus in a game against the Baltimore Orioles. This was baseball's roughest team. The Orioles were expert rule breakers. They pulled any trick to win, no matter if it hurt the other players. Honus had never played that way. When he went up to bat, he didn't know what to expect.

He connected with a pitch. It looked like a sure three-bagger. Honus took off like a streak.

The Baltimore first baseman shoved a hip in his way and sent him staggering.

Honus managed to stay on his feet. When he saw the ball still flying toward the outfield, he kept going.

The Orioles' second baseman blocked his path. Honus had to run wide around him.

By this time the third baseman had the ball. He tagged Honus so hard that he knocked him down.

Manager Clarke yelled at Honus. "You're in the big league now! You can't let anyone push you around like that!"

"All right," Honus said.

Two innings later he sent another line drive into the outfield. The first baseman was ready to shove him aside again. Honus bumped into him at full

Honus slides home in a cloud of dust.

speed. The Orioles' baseman sailed ten feet through the air before he landed.

Honus headed for second without slowing up. The second baseman had seen what happened. He jumped out of the way.

Honus reached third and crashed into the baseman there. He knocked the man flat into the dust.

Then, sitting safely on the base, Honus grinned up at Clarke.

The manager grinned back. "That's the way to play!" he said.

The news spread from team to team. "Don't play rough with Honus Wagner! You'll be sorry if you do!"

Honus was glad when other players stopped trying to push him around. He knew he could defend himself if he had to. But he didn't really like to fight, on or off the field. He just wanted to be friends with everybody.

Ballplayers had a hard life in those days, especially when they were on the road. They stayed in cheap hotels. They changed clothes in bare little shacks. After a game they often had to run for a train. They dried their sweat-soaked uniforms by hanging them out the train windows.

Many players complained. Honus didn't. He cheered up the others by telling them funny stories or playing jokes on his friends. And he didn't mind when they played jokes on him.

Once a friend said, "Would you like to go fishing tonight in my private lake?"

"Sure," Honus said.

That night the friend took him to a lake. The sky was so dark Honus could not see where he was. But he cast in his line, and soon he pulled up a fish.

Suddenly some men in police uniforms appeared. They said Honus was fishing in the lake of the city park, and that it was against the law to do that. They took him before a judge.

"Pay a $100 fine and go to jail for 30 days!" the judge said.

"But I have to play ball tomorrow!" Honus said.

Then everyone began to laugh, even the judge.

"It's all right, Honus," the judge said. "We were all playing a trick on you. Of course you can play tomorrow! And you better win too!"

Honus thought it was a good joke. He laughed too.

Honus played for Louisville until the team was broken up in 1900. Then Clarke became manager of the Pirates. He took Louisville's best players with him to Pittsburgh. Honus was one of them. He was glad to be back in Pennsylvania.

In 1901 the American League was started. The owner of the Pittsburgh Pirates knew that some of the new teams wanted Honus.

"Honus," the Pirates' owner said, "you can name your own salary if you will stay with us."

Honus at bat. For eight years the Pittsburgh slugger led the league in batting.

"Why, you don't have to give me a raise!" Honus told him. "I wouldn't think of leaving you."

Honus Wagner always told young players, "Learn to play every position, the way my brothers and I did. Then, when your chance comes, wherever it is, you'll be able to take it."

During one year with the Pirates, Honus played in seven positions!

That was one of the four years Honus helped the Pirates win the National League pennant. He also helped them beat Detroit in the 1909 World Series. In the seven games of that series, Honus hit .333. His dazzling speed let him steal six bases to tie a World Series record.

By then Honus Wagner was the team's regular shortstop. He zigzagged between second and third like a jackrabbit, making stops that looked impossible. His big hands scooped up pebbles along with the ball. His throws to first base crossed the infield like bullets. Experts say he was the greatest shortstop in major-league history.

Honus also won the National League batting championship eight times. He won the base-stealing championship five times.

Honus Wagner played with the Pirates until 1917. He was 43 years old then, and his powerful legs were slowing up. At the end of the season he retired.

But he missed the world of baseball. When the Pirates asked him to come back as a coach in 1933, he put on his old uniform again. Again he turned out for spring training and traveled with the team from city to city.

Everywhere he went, the fans crowded around to cheer the "Flying Dutchman," as they called him.

The Pirates retired his uniform when he left the team in 1952, three years before he died. They felt nobody else had the right to wear the number 33, which the great Honus Wagner had worn for so long.

Napoleon Lajoie
The Big Frenchman

by Sam and Beryl Epstein

The husky Frenchman from Woonsocket
batted with a power and grace that few
spectators ever forgot. Many believe that
Nap was the greatest of all natural hitters.

Napoleon Lajoie
The Big Frenchman

The pitcher of the New York Highlanders was worried. Cleveland had two men on base. The next Clevelander coming up to bat was Napoleon Lajoie, the man most people called Nap, or Larry.

Nap was over six feet tall. His hair was jet black. He moved with the smooth grace of a cat. His heavy bat hung from his hand as if it weighed nothing at all.

The Highlanders' catcher signaled the pitcher. "Walk him," the signal said.

The pitcher's first throw was far from the plate. Nap didn't even try to reach for it.

"Ball one!" the umpire called.

The next pitch was again far outside.

"Ball two!" the umpire said. After the third wide pitch he said, "Ball three!"

Nap Lajoie shifted his grip on the bat. Now his hands were close together at the very end of the stick.

Once more the pitcher hurled the ball. The catcher stretched far to the right, ready for another outside one. Nap's left hand dropped from his bat. His right arm reached far out, with the bat at the end of it. One-handed he swung!

Crack! The wood connected for a solid hit! Both of Nap's teammates raced home to score while he trotted easily to second.

Twice more during that game the opposing pitcher tried to walk Nap Lajoie. Each time Nap slammed the ball one-handed. Each time he got a two-base hit.

Finally the pitcher walked him by throwing four balls behind the Cleveland slugger. "Even Nap Lajoie," a baseball reporter wrote, "couldn't hit a ball with his backside."

Napoleon Lajoie was born September 5, 1875, in Woonsocket, Rhode Island. His French-Canadian parents were poor. When Napoleon was five years old, his father died. Then the family was poorer than ever.

Napoleon and his brothers and sisters went to work as soon as anyone would hire them. At first Nap did odd jobs after school. When he finished the eighth grade, he left school to work in a lumberyard.

Somehow he also found a few hours each week for a game of baseball. It was the one thing that brought real joy into his hard life. He played during his lunch hour, after work, or on Sundays.

Most of the boys he played with were as poor as he was. Their ball was usually ragged and so old that it was almost black with dirt. But they played a good game, and Napoleon Lajoie played best of all. Soon the older ballplayers in Woonsocket began to talk about him.

"Have you seen that French kid with the funny name?" a young man asked his teammate one day.

"I sure have," the teammate said. "He can really clout a ball! He told me the right way to say his last name is Laj-o-way."

"Both his names are too much for me," the first man said. "I just call him Sandy. He doesn't mind. He's got a reach like a giraffe!" he went on. "And he probably isn't even fifteen years old!"

"We could use that kid," his teammate said. "Let's ask him to play with us next Sunday."

So Napoleon Lajoie began to play with some of the regular grown-up teams around Woonsocket.

At the end of one Sunday game, a man stopped him as he was leaving the field. "I've been watching you," he said. "How would you like to play with our team, the Globe Stars?"

Napoleon was surprised. "That's a pro team, isn't it?" he said.

"Semipro," the man said. "The players pick up a few dollars every game."

By then Napoleon had a job driving a team of horses. Every day except Sunday he delivered wagon-loads of coal and wood. His salary was $7.50 a week.

"I could use a few extra dollars," he said quietly. "Sure, I'll play with you."

Nap was a member of the Globe Stars from then on. One day, when he was about twenty years old, a stranger came into the stable where Nap was hitching up his team.

"I'm Charles Marston," the man said. "I manage the Fall River team in the New England League. Would you like to play pro ball with my team? For $100 a month?" he added.

Napoleon didn't answer him for a moment. He could scarcely believe he was being offered more than three times his regular salary—and just to play ball!

"Yes, sir," he said finally. "I'd like that."

On May 1, 1896, Nap Lajoie took part in his first professional ball game. He played center field. By midseason he was batting over .400. Pitchers all over New England had learned to respect his screaming line drives.

One day a scout from the Philadelphia team of the National League turned up at Fall River. He was interested in Phil Geier, the Fall River outfielder. "How much do you want for him?" he asked Marston.

Marston thought Geier was his best player—much better than Lajoie. "Fifteen hundred dollars," he said.

Fifteen hundred dollars was a lot of money to pay for a rookie in those days. As soon as Marston had named that price, he was afraid the scout would turn him down.

"I'll tell you what I'll do," Marston said quickly. "Pay me $1,500 for Geier, and I'll throw in young Lajoie for nothing."

"All right, Marston, you've got a deal," the scout said.

So Napoleon didn't even finish his first season with Fall River. He and Geier reported to the Phillies on August 10, 1896. Two days later Napoleon was playing first base in a big-league game.

He didn't break any records that day. He did complete a double play that helped the Phillies beat Washington 9–0. But in five times at bat, he made only one hit and scored one run.

In the thirty-nine games he played for the Phillies that year, however, he made only three errors. He batted a respectable .328. When the season ended, Geier was sent back to a minor-league team. But Napoleon was offered a job for the next year at a salary of $1,800.

"I'll never have to be poor again—if I can just go on being a good ballplayer!" Nap thought. He wrote to his mother that now he could send her extra money every month.

The 1897 season was a good one for Nap. His batting average stayed in the high .300s. In one game against St. Louis, he made a single, a double, and two home runs in five times at bat!

In 1898 Colonel John Rogers, owner of the Phillies, raised Nap to $2,100 a year and shifted him to second base.

Everyone who saw Nap play at second agreed that it was his natural position. He made the most difficult catch seem easy. His throws to first traveled like bullets. Yet he never seemed to strain or hurry to get the ball there on time for a putout.

"He's so graceful!" the women fans always said. And they usually added, "He's so handsome too!"

Other players said, "Nap's playing is as easygoing as he is. He gets along with everyone."

It was true. But it was also true that when Nap left a ball park, he usually left alone. He wanted to keep in good condition, so that he could go on playing well. That was why he almost never went out with his teammates to celebrate after a victory. Instead, he got a good night's sleep.

In 1899 Colonel Rogers raised Nap's salary to $2,400 a year.

"Now I've reached the top!" Nap thought. He knew that all the major-league team owners had made an agreement. They had said that $2,400 was the highest salary they would pay any player. He was proud to think that now he and several other Phillies earned as much as any ballplayers in the world.

Then he learned that some of his highly paid teammates were also secretly receiving extra money from Colonel Rogers. One of them got as much as $600 a year over his regular salary.

"Why don't I deserve as much as any other man on the team?" Nap asked Colonel Rogers.

Rogers was angry that Nap had found out about

Connie Mack gave Nap an opportunity to star in the new American League.

the secret payments. "All right," he said. "I'll give you an extra $200 a year."

"But, Colonel—," Nap began.

"Take it or leave it!" Rogers snapped.

Nap realized that he had no choice. The National League was then the only major league in existence. He could go to another national team only if Rogers sold his contract. And he was sure Rogers wasn't going to do that. So if Nap left the Phillies, there would be no place he could go except back to a minor league— or back to delivering wood and coal.

"I'll take it," Nap said. But he wasn't happy.

Then a new major league, the American League, was started. Its owners tried to steal National League players by offering them high salaries.

"Philadelphia is going to have another major team now," a man told Nap one day. "It's the Athletics of the American League. Connie Mack, the manager, sent me to see you. He'll pay you $6,000 a year to play for him."

Nap didn't have to think very long about it. "Tell him I accept," he said.

Colonel Rogers was furious. He didn't want to lose one of his most popular players. He started a lawsuit in an effort to get Nap back.

In the meantime Nap was already playing for the Athletics. He had never played better in his life. He finished the 1901 season with the terrific batting average of .422. It won him the title of American League batting champion.

Then the lawsuit ended. The judges in a Pennsylvania state court said Napoleon must play with the Phillies of the National League. If he did not obey the order, he was subject to arrest.

"Don't worry, Nap," Connie Mack, the Athletics manager, said. "We won't let you go back to the Phillies. Our lawyers say you can't be arrested anywhere except here, in the state of Pennsylvania. Of course that means you can't play with the Athletics anymore. But the American League team in Cleveland will buy you. You can play in all its games except the ones in Pennsylvania."

So Nap joined the Cleveland team early in the 1902 season. Of course, he had to take a day off whenever Cleveland played in Pennsylvania. But he did play in eighty-seven games that year. They were enough to show Cleveland fans what he could do. His batting and fielding improved the whole team.

The next year the National League stopped fighting the new American League. Lawsuits over players came to an end. Nap knew he could go into Pennsylvania without fear of being arrested.

That year he won the American League batting championship for the second time. He won it again in 1904.

In 1905 he became Cleveland's player-manager. The fans had their own name for his team now. They called it the Cleveland Naps. "This year," they said, "Nap and the Naps will win the pennant!"

Every day the fans' dreams seemed closer to coming true. The Naps won game after game. Soon they were leading the league by a wide margin.

Then one day Nap was at his place, at second base. His team was playing the Boston Red Sox. A Red Sox player slid for the base in a cloud of dust. When the dust settled, Nap was flat on the ground. Blood was pouring from a gash on his leg. The Red Sox player had spiked him.

Nap was rushed to the hospital. His teammates and all his fans were very worried. Every day they waited for the doctors' reports. The reports grew more and more serious. Nap's wound was not healing. Blood poisoning had set in.

"He may lose his leg," the doctors said.

His teammates were doing their best to play well for Nap. But without him on the field, they didn't have their old speed and flair. Their big lead withered away.

At last came the news everyone had been hoping for. "The wound is beginning to heal," the doctors said. "Nap's leg is saved!"

But it was too late to save the Naps. They finished the season far down in the league.

For the next two seasons Nap worked hard to bring his team back up to its peak performance. He was no longer thinking so much about his own salary. Now he thought more about his players and the fans who came out to cheer them at every game.

Easygoing Nap even let his temper explode if he thought it would help his team. He did so once when the Naps were playing the Detroit Tigers. That day Nap asked the umpire for a new ball. Bringing a new ball into a game was not very common at the time. The umpire shook his head.

"But we can't hit this dead old tomato out of the infield!" Nap burst out. "It's so dirty we can't see it!"

"The Tigers played with it!" the umpire growled. "You can too!"

He was an Irishman named Tom Connolly, and he spoke with a heavy Irish brogue. "Get back to the bench!" he ordered.

"Why, you Irish immigrant!" Nap roared.

"You French blockhead!" Connolly roared back. "Get out of here!"

Nap snatched the ball from Connolly's hand and threw it over the grandstand. "There!" he shouted. "Now it's out of the game!"

"And so are you!" Connolly yelled. "Out!"

"Sure, I'll go." Nap grinned as he walked away. "But we get a new ball," he said.

The year 1908 began well for his team. Cleveland was in a fever of excitement. "We're really going to take the pennant this year!" everybody was saying.

By now the fans wanted the championship as much for Nap's sake as their own. "If there's one manager who deserves a pennant, it's our Nap," people often said.

As the season wore on, the Naps were well ahead of every team except one—the Detroit Tigers. The battle between the two was a close one. Sometimes one team was ahead. Sometimes the other.

The end was a tragedy for the Naps and Cleveland. They lost the pennant to Detroit by half a game!

Nap had put so much energy into managing that

his batting average had slipped to .289. Now he made a difficult decision.

"I'm giving up managing," he announced. "I can do more for the team by putting everything I've got into playing ball."

In 1909 he pushed his average back up to .324. His smashing drives made infielders play far back when he came to bat. Then, when he thought the infielder was back far enough, Nap bunted. Time and again he made base hits by placing a bunt that a third baseman had to run a long way to pick up.

In 1910 Nap was competing for the league batting championship with the famous Ty Cobb. An automobile company promised a car to the winner. Both men had their fans, but most of the players themselves were rooting for Nap. They didn't like Cobb. They thought that he would do anything to win.

By the last day of the season, the two men were running neck and neck. That day the Cleveland Naps were playing a doubleheader against the St. Louis Browns.

"This is the day to wrap it up, Nap!" his teammates said.

Nap hit whistling line drives. Then, when the third baseman had moved far back, he bunted. Six times he bunted, and each time he reached first safely.

That day Napoleon Lajoie made eight hits in eight times at bat! The fans cheered him until they were hoarse. Those who had been figuring the batting averages cheered loudest of all. They were sure Nap had won the championship.

Then the official figures came out. Nap's final average was .3841. Ty Cobb's was .3848. Nap had lost the championship by a narrow margin.

The owner of the automobile company said what all the fans were thinking. "Both men are champions," he said and gave a car to each of them.

Afterward the American League officials learned about something that had happened on that last day of play. It was something that might have hurt Nap's good name. They learned that the St. Louis Browns' manager had ordered his third baseman to play far back that day. The Browns' manager, in other words, had helped Nap run up that score of six safe bunts. Even Nap's opponent had wanted him to win the championship!

Fans were surprised that any manager would do such a thing. But they were sure Nap had known nothing about the plan to help him.

"He'd never be mixed up in a trick like that!" they said.

Even Ty Cobb agreed. "Lajoie, it goes without saying," he wrote later, "knew nothing of the scheme. That marvelous hitter . . . didn't need anyone's help to rank right at the top."

The Cleveland Naps never won the pennant while

Nap Lajoie—a brilliant batter and an outstanding second baseman

Nap played with them. Nap himself never won another batting championship after those early victories in 1901, 1903, and 1904. But he never lost the admiration of the fans.

In 1912, his tenth year with Cleveland, some of his admirers planned a Nap Lajoie Day in the Cleveland ball park. They presented him with a huge horseshoe, for luck. It was made of roses. Hidden among the flowers were 1,009 silver dollars the fans had collected to give him.

Nap's batting average began to slide as he grew older. From .386 in 1912 it fell to .335 the next year when Nap was 38. In 1914 it was only .285. And that year he had trouble with Cleveland's new young manager.

"He tries to tell me how to bat!" Nap told a sportswriter sadly. "Me—who was hitting over .300 when he was still in school!"

The manager let Nap go at the end of that year. Connie Mack, his old friend, hired him immediately. So Nap ended his American League career where it had begun, with the Philadelphia Athletics.

Two years later Nap, now forty-one years old, decided it was time to quit major-league ball. He no longer needed the income. He and his wife could afford a comfortable home in Cleveland and another one in Florida. The poverty of his early days was now far in the past.

But Nap still couldn't stay away from the game. For two more years he managed minor-league teams. Finally, when he was forty-three, he retired for good. He lived for another forty years. He died in February 1959.

In his later years Nap always said that the best day of his life was the day in 1937 when his name was entered in the Hall of Fame. He had gone to Cooperstown for the ceremonies. Fans cheered when he appeared. Many of them could remember watching the easy powerful swing of his bat. Many could remember the way he had streaked for a ball with the swift grace of a cat.

The bronze plaque bearing his name read, "Great hitter and most graceful and effective second baseman of his era."

"And that's the truth, Nap," more than one man told him that day.

Napoleon Lajoie had earned more than a good living out of baseball. He had earned the respect and admiration of his fellow players, and the love of fans everywhere.

Ty Cobb
The Georgia Peach

by Sam and Beryl Epstein

Fiery Ty Cobb struck fear into the hearts
of his opponents both at the plate and
on the field. His brilliant hitting and
bone-crushing slides made him a legend
on the diamond.

From *Baseball Hall of Fame: Stories of Champions*
Copyright © 1965 by Sam Epstein and Beryl Epstein

Ty Cobb
The Georgia Peach

At fourteen Tyrus Cobb was short and skinny. He weighed about 90 pounds. He wanted to grow up to be important like his handsome father, Professor Cobb. The professor ran a newspaper in Georgia, where Ty was born in 1886. The professor was a state senator too.

"Would you like to go to West Point, Ty?" Professor Cobb asked.

"I don't want to be an army officer," Ty answered.

"Then where do you want to go to college? What do you want to do?"

"I don't know," Ty said. He did know that he wanted to do something well. "I have to be the best," he told himself.

One day Ty got a chance to play baseball with the Royston Reds, his town team. As shortstop he made some good catches. He hit a clean single his first time at bat.

"I know now what I want to do!" he thought. "I want to play baseball."

Ty needed a glove to play with the Reds. He sold two books out of his father's big library to get the money to pay for it. He didn't think his father would miss them.

But the professor did. To punish Ty he wouldn't let him play ball for many months.

When Ty was seventeen, he wrote secretly to every town in the new South Atlantic Baseball League. In each letter he offered to play on the town's team. He got only one answer. It came from the Augusta team. The manager said Ty could try out during spring practice. But he would have to pay his own expenses.

Ty told his father what he had done. He asked for the money he needed.

"I don't want you to be a baseball player, Ty," his father said. "You will throw away your life if you spend it playing ball."

All Ty could say was, "I just have to go to Augusta."

Finally the professor said, "All right, son. Get it out of your system. Then you can come home and go to college." He gave Ty the money he had asked for.

Ty didn't get in a single game during spring practice. On the opening day of the season, the manager said, "One of our regular players is out today, Cobb. I'll have to put you in center field."

Ty did well and was proud of himself. He did well in the next game too. Then the regular center fielder returned.

"Sorry, Cobb," the manager said. "We can't use you anymore."

Ty was stunned. He didn't know what to do. A friend told him about a job with a semipro team in Alabama. Ty telephoned his father. "I want to take that job," he said.

"I understand, son," the professor said. "You don't want to come home a failure. Go on to Alabama."

Within a few weeks Ty had the best batting average in the little semipro league. The Augusta team had a new manager by then. The man heard about Ty's record and offered him $125 a month to come back. That was a big salary for a rookie in those days.

"I've made good!" Ty thought when he returned to Augusta. "Now I won't have to play so hard."

One day he was playing in the outfield. He had a bag of popcorn in his hand. A ball came his way. He didn't want to drop the popcorn. He missed the ball.

That night the manager said, "You could be a good ballplayer, Ty. You might even be a famous one someday. But you'll never amount to anything if you don't try harder." Ty was ashamed of himself.

By late summer he had the best batting average in his league. Suddenly the Detroit Tigers bought his contract.

Only one thing spoiled Ty's triumph. Professor Cobb had just been killed in an accident. He would never know that his son had made the major leagues.

Detroit rookie Ty Cobb slams one up the middle.

Ty drove in the two winning runs in his first game with the Tigers. The older men on the team decided to put the rookie in his place.

"Get back to the sandlot!" they told him. "This game is for men only!" They broke his bats. They made him eat all his meals alone. Nobody would room with him when they were on the road.

Ty thought they would get tired of their razzing soon. They didn't. Then he got angry.

"If I have to fight," he told himself, "I'll fight!"

He fought with his fists. Sometimes he lost, but he always came back for more.

He fought with umpires and with other players on the field too. He learned to slide into the base feet first. If he knocked the baseman down or slashed him with his spikes, he didn't care. The base paths, Ty said, belonged to the runner.

"Cobb is the toughest man in baseball," other players said. "He will do anything to win a game. But he is one of the best players in the country too."

No player ever wanted to win more than Ty Cobb. He felt angry and ill when his team lost.

Every day Cobb tried to make himself a better player. He didn't think he had much natural ability. So he practiced all the time, to make up for it. He also figured out tricks that would help him win games.

As he slid toward a base, for example, he always watched the infielder's eyes. The infielder, of course, was watching the ball. Cobb could tell from the man's eyes where the ball was coming from. Then he knew which side of the base to hit, to save himself from being tagged.

One day the Tigers were in the ninth inning of a game with the Highlanders, later called the Yankees. The score was tied, 0–0. Ty got to first base. The next batter tried a bunt, and Ty got to second. The other team expected him to stop there. He kept going. By watching the ball thrown toward third, he managed to let it hit him. The baseman couldn't catch it. Ty got safely on base. Then he stole home.

The next day the Highlanders expected him to steal bases again. Ty knew it. So he didn't try to steal a base for seven innings. The Highlanders stopped watching him closely. Then Ty took off from first on a bunt and got all the way to third!

The third baseman was so angry that he slammed the ball on the ground in a high bounce. Ty started off again as soon as he saw the ball in the air. He got home before the baseman could catch the ball and throw it.

Cobb had worked his favorite trick. He described it this way: "Upset the other team and let them beat themselves."

With tricks like that Ty Cobb broke all records for base stealing. In 1915 he stole 96 bases, a record that stood for 47 years!

Cobb was the greatest of all base runners. He is seen here sliding into base in a shower of dirt.

Cobb held his bat like a club—with his hands at least two inches apart. His powerful batting helped him make more hits, and score more runs, than any other player in baseball history.

Ty won the 1911 batting championship by upsetting his rival, Shoeless Joe Jackson of the Cleveland Indians. Jackson came from the South too. He and Ty had always been friendly.

At the start of a six-game series between the Tigers and the Indians, Jackson greeted Ty the way he always did.

"How you been, brother Ty?" Jackson asked.

Ty didn't answer him. He walked away. Jackson was puzzled. Again he spoke to Ty. Again Ty walked away. Jackson was so upset that he didn't bat as well as usual that day.

The next day the same thing happened. Jackson was even more upset.

All during the series Ty refused to speak to Jackson. Every day Jackson's batting grew worse.

When the series was over, Ty spoke to Jackson again. "Hello, Joe!" he said.

Jackson didn't know Ty had been pulling one of his tricks. Jackson's batting average that year was .408. Ty's was .420.

Every winter Ty Cobb walked 20 or 30 miles a day to keep himself in shape. He wore pieces of metal in his shoes to make them heavy. Then, when he put his playing shoes on in the spring, they felt so light he ran with extra speed.

Cobb always held his hands at least two inches apart on the bat. When he was a skinny boy, that was the only way he could get enough strength behind his swing. Later he found the grip was just right for punching out singles and doubles and placing hits. When he and Honus Wagner met for the first time, in the 1909 World Series, photographers crowded around the two stars.

"Come on, let's get the two batting champs together in the batting box!" the photographers said.

Ty and Honus didn't even hear them at first. They were too busy talking about something they had just discovered: big, awkward Honus and wiry, fast Ty Cobb held their bats in exactly the same way!

Cobb could bat the "dead" ball used when he started to play. He could bat the lively, bouncy "jackrabbit" ball used after 1920. No other batter made records with both balls, as he did. He was the American League batting champion twelve times!

In 1911 Cobb was named the league's Most Valuable Player for the year. He was the first choice of every expert voting. This high honor was paid only to Cobb and to Babe Ruth.

Ty Cobb played with the Tigers from 1905 to 1926. He also managed the team from 1921 to 1926. He was more than 40 years old then. But Connie Mack, one of baseball's smartest managers, knew Cobb was still a valuable player. He hired him to play with the Athletics. That year Cobb stole 22 bases and hit .357 in 134 games.

Altogether Ty Cobb played 3,033 games, more than any other major-league baseball player. His plaque in the Hall of Fame says that he "created or equalled more major league records than any other player."

Ty Cobb had won his boyhood ambition. He grew up to be somebody important. His home town, Royston, was proud of the Georgia Peach, as Ty's fans called him. Royston was also proud of the hospital Cobb built there and the fund he set up to help students go to college.

Cobb was able to build that hospital and set up that fund because he had broken one more record. By investing his money wisely, he had become the first millionaire player in baseball.

Tris Speaker
The Gray Eagle

by Sam and Beryl Epstein

The kid from Texas just had to play
baseball! He became Boston's great Gray
Eagle—a powerful batter and one of the
greatest outfielders of all time.

Tris Speaker

The Gray Eagle

Young Tris Speaker had a strong right arm. He never missed a chance to throw with it.

Every night he had to bring the cows back to their barn behind the family house in the little Texas town of Hubbard City. On the way he picked up stones and threw them as far as he could. He played baseball with the boys his own age. He always wanted to play with the older boys too.

When he was ten years old, he hung around the field where the high school boys played. "Can I get into the game?" he asked.

"Sure," he was often told. "You can really throw, Tris. You're a good batter too."

Tris's mother sometimes let him visit a ranch near Hubbard City. It was owned by one of his relatives. There, Tris's cowboy friends showed him how to throw a lariat. They also showed him how to ride. Soon he rode so well that he could help break wild broncos.

One day Tris was riding a bronco when the animal suddenly bucked. Tris flew over his head and landed with a thud. The pain in his right arm was so sharp that it brought tears to his eyes.

"The arm is broken, Tris," the doctor said when Tris was taken to see him. "You won't be playing any more baseball this year."

Tris refused to believe him.

"Oh, yes, I will, sir!" he said. "Maybe I can't bat for a while. But I'll learn to throw with my left arm."

And he did. Soon his left arm was stronger than his right arm. He went on throwing left-handed even after his broken arm was healed. He began to bat left-handed too.

He was captain of the baseball team in high school. Then he went to college in Fort Worth, about 100 miles from his home. He started to study banking. But the thing he liked best at school was playing on the college baseball team.

Soon he decided that he did not want to be a banker and to sit at a desk all his life. He left college and took a job at a cottonseed mill back home in Hubbard City. The mill closed down for a few months every summer. That gave Tris plenty of time to play baseball.

His widowed mother was sorry Tris wasn't going to finish college. But she was glad to have Tris at home with her again. She called him her "baby" because he was the youngest of her eight children.

Tris began to pitch for a team from the larger town of Corsicana, not far from Hubbard. "That

Tris Speaker got his start in small-town baseball
games like this one.

Speaker kid is good enough to be a professional,"
many people said.

"I wonder if they're right," Tris thought. He decided to find out.

He wrote letters to managers of some of the professional teams in Texas. He told them he was a
good pitcher, and that he was pretty good at bat
too. "I'd like a chance to try out for your team,"
he said.

No one answered his letters.

Then one afternoon a stranger in a horse and
buggy stopped to watch the Corsicana team play.
He watched Tris pitch his side to victory. Tris also
batted two home runs.

"You, boy—the pitcher!" the stranger called when the game ended. "I want to talk to you."

Tris ran over to the man seated in the buggy.

"I'm Doak Roberts," the stranger said. "I own the Cleburne Club team of the North Texas League."

The Cleburne Club manager was one of the men Tris had written to!

"I'm sure glad to meet you, Mr. Roberts!" Tris said, jumping up on the hub of the buggy wheel. His spikes scratched the fresh paint on the hub, but Tris was too excited to notice.

Mr. Roberts looked at the scratches. Then he looked at the tall lean boy with the tanned face. He remembered the way Tris had pitched. "Would you like to try out for my team?" he asked.

"I sure would, Mr. Roberts!" Tris said.

"All right," Roberts said. "Here is a dollar for your train fare. Go to Waco tomorrow and ask at the hotel there for my manager, Ben Shelton. Tell him I sent you."

Tris was at the hotel at 6:30 the next morning. He went to the door of Ben Shelton's room and knocked on it.

"Mr. Shelton!" he called out. "Mr. Roberts sent me to try out for your team!"

"Do you know what time it is?" an angry voice shouted. "Go away! I'll see you downstairs when I get up."

Tris had to wait three hours before Shelton came down. The man was still angry, but he let Tris go with him to the practice field.

Tris warmed up for half an hour. He pitched for the team's batting practice. He shagged flies.

"I'll let you pitch today," Shelton said to Tris at game time. "Warm up."

"I don't have to warm up," Tris said. "I'm hot now!"

Shelton glared at him as he took up his own position at first base.

Tris did pretty well that day. In the bottom of the ninth inning, Cleburne was ahead, 2–1.

Tris hurled the ball. A batter connected and started for first. The runner on first streaked for second. Shelton scooped the ball up from the ground. He tried to tag the batter as he touched base and ran on.

The umpire signaled that the runner was safe, and the man kept on going. So did the player who had been on first. Shelton still held the ball. He was sure the umpire had made a mistake. He was keeping the ball as a protest.

Both runners raced across the plate, one right behind the other. The game was over. Cleburne had lost, 3–2. Tris told Shelton what he thought of him.

The next morning Roberts was in Waco. Soon he went looking for Tris. "They tell me you insulted my manager," he said.

"All I said was that he was a butter-brained bum for holding that ball instead of throwing it home," Tris said.

Roberts decided the young man had courage as well as skill. He also thought Tris had to learn a few lessons.

"If you will apologize to Mr. Shelton, I'll hire you," he said.

Tris thought about it, "Yes, sir," he said. "I will apologize."

"I'll pay you fifty dollars a month," Roberts said. That was about the usual salary for a minor-league rookie at that time.

Tris made twice as much at the mill. But with the Cleburne team he would be a real professional ballplayer.

"That will be fine, sir," he said.

"For the first month, however," Roberts said, "I'll pay you only forty dollars. I'll use the other ten dollars for painting my buggy. Your spikes scratched it. Your money will have to pay for fixing it."

Tris grinned. "Yes, sir," he said. "That seems fair."

Shelton put Tris on the mound the next day, against Fort Worth. Almost every time Tris pitched a ball, a batter connected. Fort Worth got twenty-two hits. All of them were two-baggers or better.

"You're doing fine, kid," Shelton growled at him angrily. "They haven't gotten a single off you yet."

It was a bad beginning for a professional career. But it didn't destroy Tris's faith in himself.

It was still early in the season when a Cleburne fielder was hurt. Shelton had to replace him.

"Try me," Tris said. "I'm a good outfielder."

"Well, you're not much good on the mound," Shelton said. "All right. Let's see what you can do out there."

Tris was eighteen years old that spring day in the year 1906. He was taking his first step toward winning a place in the Hall of Fame. His plaque there calls him "the greatest center fielder of his day." Many experts say he was the best center fielder in the history of baseball.

From that day on Tris's name began to pop up in newspaper stories. The stories all said what a fine outfielder he was. They said he was a good hitter too. He helped his team to one victory after another. The Cleburne Club won the North Texas League pennant that year.

At the end of the season, Tris went back home to his mother and his job at the mill. He showed his mother all those newspaper stories.

"Read them, mom," he said. "You'll be proud of me."

She pushed them away. "I'm not interested in baseball, Tris," she said. "I'm just glad to have my baby home again."

That winter Roberts bought the Houston Club and offered Tris a place on it at twice his old salary. But Mrs. Speaker didn't want Tris to be away for the whole summer.

"But it's what I love, mom," Tris said. "I just have to go."

She couldn't hold him. Tris went. He played well for Houston. In the 1907 season he took part in 118 games for a batting average of .314.

The president of the Boston Red Sox heard about Tris and wanted to buy him. Roberts agreed. The Red Sox sent Tris a contract.

Tris hurried home with it. "Mom!" he said. "The Boston team of the American League is buying me for $750!"

"How can anybody buy you?" Mrs. Speaker demanded. "You're not a slave!"

"You don't understand, mom!" Tris said. "This means I'll be in the big league!" Then he added, "But you have to sign my contract because I'm not of age yet. So please sign here, mom."

"I will not sign any paper that treats you like a slave," Mrs. Speaker said. "Anyway, why should you go all the way to Boston when you have a good home right here?"

Tris had to plead with her for a long time. Finally she put her name on the paper that gave Tris Speaker his big chance.

He spent the last few weeks of that season with the Boston team. But most of the time he was sitting on the bench. During spring training the next year, at Little Rock, Arkansas, the manager took him aside.

"The Little Rock team will take one of our players as part of our rent for using their grounds," he said. "So I'm leaving you here, Speaker."

Tris felt his heart sink. He was back in a minor league! And there was nothing he could do about it. "Maybe mom was right," he thought. "Maybe I'm nothing but a slave."

But he knew he couldn't give up baseball. "I'll show Boston!" he promised himself.

Little Rock won the Southern League pennant that season. Everyone agreed that Tris was the best player in the league. He led it in hits and runs with a batting average of .350.

Near the end of the year, the Little Rock manager said, "I'm getting some fine offers for you from the big leagues, Tris. Pittsburgh wants you. So does Cincinnati."

Tris tried to feel pleased, but he had hoped that Boston would want him back again. Then Boston heard about those offers.

"Speaker is only on loan to you," the Boston manager told the Little Rock manager. "Return him immediately."

Soon Speaker was being cheered as one of the finest players on the Boston team. He was still a powerful batter. But it was his fielding that was making him famous.

He always played closer to second base than any other man in the game. "Why do you play so close?" many people asked him.

Speaker explained. "I have found," he said, "that not more than one in six of the balls driven to the outfield go beyond the outfielder. The rest strike in front of him. I have found it best to be on hand

Boston fans jammed the stands to root for the Red Sox and the powerful young hitter from Texas.

for the short hits and to take a chance on the long ones."

The Red Sox pitcher, Smokey Joe Wood, once told how Speaker handled a long one. Smokey Joe was Speaker's roommate and friend.

"At the crack of the bat," he said, "he'd be off with his back to the infield. Then he'd turn and glance over his shoulder at the last minute and catch the ball so easy it looked like there was nothing to it, nothing at all. Nobody else was even in the same league with him."

In 1912 Speaker was judged the most valuable player in the American League. His batting average had been .383. He had made 222 hits in 153 games. Nine were home runs. And his fielding had led to many Red Sox victories.

That year Boston romped home with the pennant. Then the team met the New York Giants in the World Series. It was called "the most exciting, nerve-wracking series ever played."

A huge crowd filled the New York Polo Grounds field on the opening day, October 8. When Speaker batted a ball into the stands during practice, more than 35,000 people rose to cheer him.

The Giants got an early two-run lead, but Joe Wood pitched the Sox to a 4–3 victory.

After the game the players and hundreds of their fans left for Boston by special train. The same train carried them back and forth between Boston and New York each evening during the series. It was always jammed. It was always noisy. One group of fans, called the Royal Rooters, sang all the way. The mayor of Boston was among them.

The next day the teams played in Boston's Fenway Park. At the end of nine innings, the score was tied 5–5. In the first half of the tenth inning, the Giants got another run. Then, in the second half, Speaker came to bat.

The Giants' pitcher, the famous Christy Mathewson, sent a sizzler toward the plate. Tris swung and connected. It was a home run! Once more the score was tied. It was still tied at 6–6 when the game was called because of darkness.

Back in New York, the next day, Speaker rode around the field in the new car he had won as the league's most valuable player. As always, his fielding was brilliant. But that day the Giants won, 2–1. The series was tied.

The Giants won the next two games. Boston won the two games after that. Again the series was tied.

The eighth game was played in Boston. In the tenth inning the Giants were ahead, 2–1. Once more the great Mathewson was pitching for them. Speaker came up to bat with two men on base. He popped up a foul fly. The Giants' first baseman started for it.

Then Christy Mathewson shouted to his catcher to

Southpaw Tris Speaker was a hard-hitting batter and a remarkable outfielder—one of the greatest glove men in baseball history.

make the catch. The first baseman stopped. The ball dropped into the coach's box at first base before the catcher could reach it.

Young Tris Speaker gave a triumphant shout. "There goes your World Series!" he called out to the veteran Mathewson.

Tris was right. He plastered the next ball for a single that drove in the tying run. Another Boston runner went to third base. On the next play, that runner made it to home plate, and the ball game was over.

The Boston Red Sox had won their World Series. Tris Speaker was the hero of Boston and of the whole nation.

Speaker had also set a new mark for batters to shoot at. He topped the fifty-one doubles Napoleon Lajoie had batted in two years earlier. Tris doubled fifty-three times during the season.

Not long afterward a new baseball league, the Federal League, was being formed. Its owners offered him a high salary if he would leave the Red Sox. Tris told the Red Sox about the offer.

"We'll meet it," the owner said.

So Tris stayed with the Red Sox at a salary of $18,000 a year. He was probably the highest paid ballplayer of that time.

In 1915 the Red Sox won the pennant again. That time they played Philadelphia in the World Series.

Woodrow Wilson threw out the opening ball at the second game of the 1915 World Series.

Philadelphia won the first game, 3–1. The following day President Woodrow Wilson watched Speaker help his team to a 2–1 victory. That was the first time an American president had come to a series game. President Wilson threw out the opening ball.

In the third game Speaker's triple gave his team another 2–1 win. The Red Sox also won the next two games and took the series.

Tris Speaker was now more famous than ever. He had a new nickname too. He was given it one day when someone called out "Speaker has spoke!" every time Tris's bat hit the ball. So the fans called him "Spoke."

Sportswriters had another name for him. They called him the "Gray Eagle." His hair was already gray, and he was as swift as a big bird pouncing on its prey. One writer said, "He was all 'eagle' in roaming the outfield and making seemingly impossible catches."

Tris Speaker talked in a gruff voice that rumbled like thunder. But his words were always warm and friendly. He was never too busy to visit boys' camps and hospitals for children.

"I don't think Spoke ever had an enemy!" Smokey Joe Wood said.

In 1916 Speaker was twenty-eight years old. The Red Sox owner thought Spoke's best baseball days were over. The new Federal League had failed and could no longer try to win Speaker away from the Sox. So the Sox owner offered Tris a new contract for only $9,000—just half the salary he had been getting.

Speaker refused to sign the contract. The Red Sox traded him to the Cleveland Indians. This was the team that had been known as the Naps a few years earlier when its manager and star was Napoleon Lajoie.

Tris immediately proved what a mistake the Red Sox had made. That year his batting average was .386. He won the American League batting championship from Detroit's great hitter, Ty Cobb.

Cleveland fans rejoiced. They remembered how Nap Lajoie had battled Cobb for that championship. That time Cobb had won.

"Now the mighty Cobb has fallen," the fans said. "And our Tris toppled him!"

In 1919 Speaker became player-manager of the Indians. He brought in new players. He worked hard with them. Soon they caught some of his own spirit.

They never forgot what he did one day when they were playing the Chicago White Sox. Joe Jackson of the White Sox had driven a tremendous smash to right center. Tris reached it just as it was about to hit the wall.

He struck the wall so hard that he was knocked out. But as he lay unconscious on the ground, the ball was still in his hand. He had saved the game.

In 1920 the Indians captured the pennant. With Speaker they had finally won the victory they had fought for under Nap Lajoie. Then they went on to beat Brooklyn in the World Series by taking five games out of seven.

After the final winning run, thousands of fans flooded onto the field. "Spoke!" they roared. "Spoke!" Tris Speaker had brought them their first pennant and their first World Series victory.

Tris made his way through the crowd to a little white-haired woman sitting in a box.

"This was what I meant, mom," he said, as he hugged his mother. "This was why I had to play ball."

That day, at last, Mrs. Speaker told reporters she was proud of her son.

Speaker was thirty-nine when he left Cleveland. He was married by then. He had proved he could be a successful businessman between baseball seasons. Even so he didn't leave the game.

He played for a year with the Washington Senators and a year with the Philadelphia Athletics. He managed the Newark team of the International League for two years. Then he became a baseball broadcaster.

Even at the age of seventy, when his steel business had made him a rich man, Speaker was still a ballplayer at heart. He was looking forward to the next spring training season. He planned to spend it as a batting instructor with Cleveland.

During a visit to his old home in Texas, on December 8, 1958, he died suddenly of a heart attack.

"Texas put him in its Hall of Fame," a newspaper said after the great ballplayer's death. "He was as much a part of Cleveland as Lake Erie. Boston called him its own."

The whole world of baseball had loved Tris Speaker, the Gray Eagle. It had loved him almost as much as he had loved the game he played all his life.

Rogers Hornsby
Hard-Driving Rajah

by Ann Finlayson

Baseball meant everything to the Rajah!
He worked hard to become the greatest
right-handed batter in baseball history.
Hornsby's amazing 1924 batting average
of .424 is the highest ever recorded in
modern times.

Rogers Hornsby
Hard-Driving Rajah

Manager Miller Huggins of the St. Louis Cardinals saw his new shortstop approaching. Rogers Hornsby was a good-looking Texas boy, tall and lanky. He always said what he thought—no punches pulled, everything out in the open.

"Hug," he asked frankly, "what are my chances for next year?"

Manager Huggins wasn't sure what answer to give the earnest nineteen-year-old. For the last three weeks of the 1915 season, Rogers had been trying out for a place on the St. Louis team. He had not been playing up to major-league standards.

"Well, Rogers," the manager said finally, "you've got plenty of fire and ambition, and I like that. But there's not enough weight behind your batting swing. These major-league pitchers have you handcuffed."

"Does that mean I'm fired?"

"Not exactly. To tell you the truth, Rogers, I think you need to be farmed out until you get more weight and seasoning."

"Farmed out?" repeated Hornsby.

"That's right. I'm telling you for your own good."

When Huggins said "farmed out," he meant "returned to the minor leagues." He felt that young Hornsby needed a year or two of experience before he entered major-league competition. But the Texas boy thought the manager was talking about a real farm.

"I'll see what I can do," he promised.

He walked away, his mind turning over rapidly. There was his uncle's farm in Caldwell County, Texas. He'd go there and work hard, and maybe next spring he'd make good.

He *had* to make good. The only thing Rogers Hornsby had ever wanted to do with his life was to be a big-league ballplayer. And the only way he knew how to get there was to work.

His mother had taught him that, back in West Texas where he was born in 1896. There had been five children in the Hornsby family and not much money. Everybody had had to work hard.

But the Hornsbys all played hard too, and their favorite game was baseball. Rogers would walk five miles or more to get into a game. Sometimes he played in two or three games in one day. "Baseball, baseball," his mother often sighed. "That boy thinks of nothing else."

Rogers was ten when he got his first job. He worked as a messenger boy for a local packinghouse.

To his delight the company had a baseball team, and he wheedled the players into making him bat boy. Sometimes they even let him play.

"You know, that kid is *good*," the team captain said one day. After that, when a player had to miss a game, they let Rogers fill in. By the time he was twelve, he had played almost every position on the team.

The Hornsbys were living in Fort Worth by then. "Mom, I need a baseball uniform," Rogers told his mother one day. "I just joined the North Side Athletics."

"Another team?" cried Mrs. Hornsby.

"Yes, I need the practice." The boy looked at her with a serious expression. "Mom," he said slowly, "do you think I could be a big leaguer someday?"

"Why, I don't know, Rogers," she answered. "But if you have talent, work is what will bring it out."

Rogers nodded, taking the words to heart.

Mrs. Hornsby could see how much the game meant to him. She found some old blue flannel and made it into uniforms for the team. When Rogers needed sliding pads, she cut up an old quilt. She encouraged him.

Rogers drove himself hard. When he was eighteen, he was given a tryout with a Class D team in a small town. That team soon folded, but Rogers was sold to the club at Denison, Texas. He was still raw and clumsy and overeager. He made an error in every two or three games. But he worked hard to correct his faults.

He was playing shortstop at Denison when a Cardinals' scout first saw him. The scout was impressed with his dash and drive. So, in September 1915, Rogers reported to St. Louis for his big chance. He had tried hard, but he wasn't surprised when Miller Huggins said he needed farming out.

Rogers spent the winter of 1916 on his uncle's farm. He did chores, tended livestock, and mended fences. He slept twelve hours every night. He ate eggs and fried chicken and biscuits. And in his spare time he worked at his batting swing.

At spring training time, Rogers reported to the Cardinals' camp 25 pounds heavier. Miller Huggins hardly recognized him. When Rogers explained what he had done, the manager laughed. "Maybe your idea of 'farmed out' is better than mine," he admitted. "Here's a bat. Get up there and show me what you can do."

Rogers stepped up to the plate. He had been advised to choke up on the bat. "Only really powerful hitters can swing from the tip," Manager Huggins had often told him. Now, however, Rogers decided to do it his own way.

He slid his hands down to the end of the bat. He

stood as far from the plate as possible, his heels touching the rim of the batter's box.

"All right, blaze one in there," he called to the pitcher.

The pitcher grinned at Huggins and pitched a hot one right down the middle.

Rogers stepped into it, his husky arms bringing the bat around hard and fast. There was a mighty *crack!*

Huggins's jaw dropped. So did the pitcher's. The little white ball was still rising as it cleared the outfield fence.

Rogers tried it again and again, while Huggins watched. The extra weight had indeed given young Hornsby added power. Finally Huggins called, "All right, kid, that's enough for today." He said nothing more about sending Rogers back to the minor leagues.

By the end of the 1916 season, Rogers Hornsby had a batting average of .313 and was in the big leagues to stay.

Once Rogers was sure that he was a full-fledged Cardinal, he made up his mind to become the best batter around. Day after day he worked at his batting. He listened to Manager Huggins's advice, but in the end Rogers developed a style that was like nobody else's.

"Look at Hornsby," said a St. Louis fan, watching him play. "How can he hit, standing so far back in the box? Most batters crowd the plate."

"When the pitch comes," he explained, "I know just where to expect it. Then I can step in and get my full power behind the swing." Unlike many power hitters, Rogers could hit to all fields.

He batted right-handed, which was supposed to be a slight handicap. First base is one step farther away from a right-hander than from a left. But Rogers refused to switch.

"Most great batters hit left," he was warned.

He shrugged it off. "This is the right way for me."

Rogers put everything he had into baseball. He would not play golf, because he was afraid it would hurt his swing. He avoided movies to protect his eyesight. He did not drink or smoke, because he wanted to keep in top condition.

He worked to improve his fielding. He tried playing second base and third base and even the outfield. Finally he settled down for good at second base. Soon the awkward boy who had been troubled by errors was being called baseball's finest second baseman.

"Look how he makes that across-the-chest throw!" one sportswriter said to another. "That's one of the toughest throws in baseball."

"Hornsby sure rips it off smooth as silk," his friend agreed.

In 1918 Miller Huggins went to the New York Yankees. He was replaced the following season by another great manager, Branch Rickey. Rickey liked

The mighty Rajah follows through on a solid hit. Hornsby is known as the best right-handed batter of all time.

to lecture to his team, diagramming plays on a blackboard. Rogers had great respect for both Huggins and Rickey, but he had his own ideas about how the game should be played.

"You have to drive every minute," he told a teammate. "You have to fight for every run."

Rogers studied every angle of the game, every technique. He made himself familiar with the weak points and strong points of every player. But he never neglected his batting. Hard years of practice slowly built up his average. In 1920, when he had boosted it to the .370 mark, he won his first batting championship.

Up till then, few people outside St. Louis had been interested in Rogers Hornsby. But nobody can ignore a champion. "There he is," fans pointed out to one another. "Look at him swing that bat!"

"Come on, Hornsby!" the Cards' rooters cheered. "Rogers the Rajah!! You're king of batters in this league!"

The name spread, and soon fans were saying, "Here comes the Rajah! The Rajah will knock in this run. Come on, Rajah!"

Rogers lived up to his new nickname. In 1921 he pushed his average up to .397. The following year he hit .401. That magic .400 mark had been topped only twelve times in major-league history. But Rogers was not content to do it once. Twice more he racked up averages in the .400s. In 1924 the Texas slugger finished the season with an average of .424. Nearly half a century later, that figure still stands as the modern record.

On May 31, 1925, Hornsby was called into the Cardinals' head office. "Rogers," said the club owner, "Rickey is moving up to the business end of the game. How would you like to be manager in his place?"

The husky Texan stared at his boss. "But I'm just a hitter, a slugger."

"We think you're a lot more than that. How about trying it?"

Rogers didn't need to think it over for long. "I want the job," he said.

Grimly the new manager considered his problems. The Cardinals had never won a pennant. In early 1925 they were in last place. Branch Rickey had good ideas, but his leadership was weak. All along, Rogers had thought the Cardinals needed push. Now he was going to see that they got it.

Hornsby became a driving leader, demanding the best from his players. One day an outfielder dawdled and missed a catch. At the end of the inning, the manager cornered the man. "You're playing rotten ball," Rogers told him bluntly. "If I don't see some improvement, you're off the club."

He did see some improvement. But only Rogers could say things like that. He let no outsiders interfere with his authority. When a club owner tried to give him some baseball advice, Rogers said, "Listen, you take care of the stock market, and I'll take care of the team."

Many people resented this outspokenness. Others believed that his methods were good for the team.

The Cardinals finished the 1925 season in fourth place. Their new manager hit .403 and won his sixth batting championship in a row. St. Louis fans began to get their hopes up. "Wait till next year," they promised one another. "If the Rajah keeps on this way, we'll have that pennant yet."

Rogers' hopes were high too, but he knew it wouldn't be easy. The Pittsburgh Pirates, Cincinnati Reds, and New York Giants had all finished ahead of St. Louis the previous year. All three were still strong contenders in 1926. And the Cardinals had an additional handicap: the team management insisted on their playing exhibition games between regular season games.

"My men are worn out," Rogers protested with his usual directness. "They need to rest on off days."

"We need the money," the club owner answered.

"The best way to make money is to have a pennant-winning team. How can we win with worn-out players?"

"I'm sorry, Rogers. The extra games have to be played."

Another man might have used the exhibition games as an excuse for failure. But Rogers responded to every setback with more drive and greater determination. "We'll show them," he told his men angrily. "We'll win that pennant in spite of them."

He made some changes in the lineup and saw that everyone trained hard. In June he talked the front office into buying Grover Cleveland Alexander from the Cubs. "Old Pete" Alexander was one of the greatest pitchers of all time. In three separate seasons he had won more than 30 games, a tremendous feat. In six others he had won more than 20. He tied the immortal Christy Mathewson in total number of games won. In 1926 Alexander was 39 and nearing the end of his pitching career. But Hornsby thought he could help the Cardinals.

The Cardinals started out slowly, but Rogers drove them to be better. He was the heart of the team. He beat out hits, scrambled after double plays, and stretched singles into doubles with daring base running. Most of all, his big bat always seemed to be ready when a hit was needed most.

"Every play counts," he told his players. "I don't want any man on my team who won't give everything he's got."

By midsummer the Giants were out of the running. Throughout August, the race was between the Pirates and the Reds, with the Cardinals slowly catching up. On August 31, St. Louis took first place and held it for four days. On September 4, they lost it to the Reds. The next day, they took it back.

Gradually the Pirates faded out. The last three weeks of the season turned into a neck and neck race between the Cardinals and the Cincinnati Reds.

"This is undoubtedly one of the most sensational races the major circuits have ever known," marveled a veteran sports reporter.

On September 13, the St. Louis Cardinals announced that the club was accepting orders for World Series tickets. Perhaps it was too soon. That same day, the team lost a fourteen-inning heartbreaker, and the pennant race was tied.

The next day the Cardinals had to play an exhibition game in New Haven, Connecticut. Between innings, Rogers rushed to the radio for news of the Cincinnati-Brooklyn game. "Come on, Bums!" he rooted. But the Reds won and took the lead.

Two days later, a determined Hornsby led his team onto the field in Philadelphia for a doubleheader. "The Reds are only playing one game today," he told them. "If we win both ends of this one, we'll be even again."

The Cardinals poured onto the field, Hornsby's reminder ringing in their ears. Restlessly they waited for their chance, and in the third inning it came. One man hit safely, then another, then a third. Before the inning was over, the Cardinals had piled up twelve runs off five pitchers. The game ended 23–3. The second game was another massacre, 10–2.

The Reds had also won, so the race was tied.

On September 17, St. Louis beat the Phillies once more, while the Reds were losing. The Cardinals were back on top, and there they stayed.

On September 24, Hornsby and his men clinched the pennant.

St. Louis went wild with joy. It was raining hard that day, but no one cared. Cars jammed the streets. Fans threw confetti and straw hats out of windows.

Paper streamers hung from telephone wires. Factory whistles blew. Police and fire sirens blared. Strangers danced together in the street.

The weary ballplayers grinned at one another.

But to hard-driving Rogers the job was only half done. "We still have the World Series to win," he pointed out bluntly.

The American League champions that year were the mighty New York Yankees. Their lineup rang with ominous names: Babe Ruth, Tony Lazzeri, Bob Meusel, Lou Gehrig. Their manager was Rogers' old boss, Miller Huggins. All the experts predicted a Yankee victory.

"This powerful New York team will steamroller the Cardinals," one reporter wrote confidently.

But Hornsby thought the Cardinals could win. "We've fought hard all summer against heavy odds," he told newsmen. "You can bet your life we're not going to stop fighting now."

Rogers also had a personal misfortune to battle. Just before the series started, his mother fell dangerously ill in Texas. Years before, she had helped him get started by making his first uniform. Now she refused to let her last illness draw Rogers home. "Tell him to stay with his team and win," she said firmly just before she died.

The funeral was postponed, and Rogers stayed with the Cardinals.

The Yankees were a mighty foe! New York's Tony Lazzeri is seen here scoring in the 1926 Series.

The series opened on October 2, in Yankee Stadium. The Yankees won the first game. St. Louis took the second and third games, and the Yankees won the fourth and fifth. When the Cardinals evened the score by winning the sixth game, fans were wild with excitement.

The seventh and final game was played in New York. "Here comes Ruth!" cried fans as the great hitter appeared at the plate. The Babe swung, there was a *crack!* and 40,000 New Yorkers screamed with delight.

"A home run! We're ahead!"

But the Cardinals caught up. In the fourth inning, they scored three runs. Two innings later, the Yankees got one more, making the score 3–2. Then came the seventh inning, one of the most memorable in the history of baseball.

Jesse Haines, the Cardinals' pitcher, had a blister on his finger. "Think you can finish the game?" Hornsby asked him anxiously.

"I think so. Let me try."

It was a bad situation, but Hornsby didn't know what else to do. All his pitchers were tired. His best man, "Old Pete" Alexander, had already won two series games. "All right, Jesse. We'll see how it goes."

Haines managed to get two men out. But then his control went. He walked Ruth, Gehrig, and Combs, the center fielder, filling the bases. The next man up was rugged Tony Lazzeri.

Rogers walked over to the mound. "I'm sorry, Jesse, but I have to pull you out."

He signaled to the bullpen. He had made a risky decision. Alexander had pitched only the day before. But if any man could save the Cardinals, he was it.

"Old Pete" ambled out to the mound to meet his boss. "Well, you can see the situation," Rogers said. "The bases are full, and Lazzeri is up. Lazzeri's runs-batted-in record is nearly as good as Babe Ruth's."

"Old Pete" nodded. "I'll handle Lazzeri."

The first pitch was a strike. The second one looked

good to Lazzeri, and he swung. The ball went streaking toward the left-field wall, and Yankee fans rose with a shriek. But it landed foul.

"Old Pete" set himself. This was the big one. He took the sign and went into his windup. The pitch was a low curve. Lazzeri braced himself and stood up to it. *Whiff!* The umpire jerked up his thumb.

"Old Pete" Alexander had struck him out. And Rogers' faith in the aging pitcher had paid off.

For two more innings, Alexander kept the mighty Yankees from scoring. When the game ended, the St. Louis Cardinals were world champions.

Rogers Hornsby, with his big bat and his hard driving, had made baseball history.

Hornsby continued to make baseball history. Over the years the Rajah managed four different major-league baseball teams. As late as 1952, he was brought out of retirement to build up the St. Louis Browns.

But it was as a hitter that Rogers Hornsby won his greatest personal fame. His lifetime average of .358 was topped only by that of left-hander Ty Cobb. And only the immortal Cobb shared Hornsby's feat of three times topping .400.

"Rogers Hornsby," say the sportswriters, "was the greatest right-handed batsman in the history of the game."

Babe Ruth

Sultan of Swat

by Sam and Beryl Epstein

The one and only Babe was the mightiest slugger of them all. Fans packed the stands to see the colorful Sultan of Swat wallop the ball out of the park. Baseball was never the same again!

From *Baseball Hall of Fame: Stories of Champions*
Copyright © 1965 by Sam Epstein and Beryl Epstein

Babe Ruth

Sultan of Swat

Babe Ruth's real name was George Herman Ruth, but nobody called him that. Newspaper reporters called him the Home Run King or the Sultan of Swat or the Bambino. Men who played with him called him the Big Guy. His fans called him Babe, or the Babe.

When they saw him on the street, they would shout, "Hiya, Babe!" The Babe always answered. He loved everybody, and everybody loved him. He especially loved children.

Once during a World Series a doctor asked the Babe to visit a sick boy in a New Jersey hospital.

"He will not even try to get better," the doctor said. "I'm afraid he will die. But you're his hero, Babe. If he could see you, maybe he would try to get well."

The next morning Babe Ruth left New York and drove to New Jersey. In the hospital he sat down beside the boy's bed. He told him baseball stories. He gave him a bat and a ball.

"Listen to your radio this afternoon, Johnny," the Babe said as he left. "I'm going to hit a homer just for you."

That afternoon the Yankees played the St. Louis team. Babe did what he had said he would do. He hit a home run.

The boy began to get better. Soon he was well again. He always said he owed his life to Babe Ruth.

Babe was born in Baltimore, Maryland, in 1895. He was one of five children. His parents were poor and had very little time for him. He ran wild in the streets. When he was seven years old, he was put into St. Mary's School. This was a home for orphans and for children, like Babe, who got into trouble.

At St. Mary's he learned to play ball. Soon he was the best player in the school. He could play any position. The school's coach brought the manager of a minor-league Baltimore team to see him. The manager hired Babe immediately.

Babe pitched in his first professional game on April 22, 1914. He was a tall, awkward nineteen-year-old, with a big body and thin legs. He stood and walked pigeon-toed. He threw left-handed. In that first game he pitched a shutout. He also hit a two-bagger. His team won, 6–0.

The Boston Red Sox bought Ruth later that season. During the next four years he became a famous pitcher. In two of those years he won 23 games a season. He pitched against the great Walter Johnson in eight games and won six of them. He helped the Red Sox win three pennants.

In his early Red Sox days, the Babe was already
thrilling fans with his out-of-the-park hits.

The Red Sox manager was Ed Barrow, the man who discovered Honus Wagner. Barrow knew he had another great player in Babe Ruth. Then Babe proved he could bat as well as he could pitch. In an exhibition game in 1919, he hit a ball 597 feet. This is over a tenth of a mile!

"You can't keep a batter like that out of the line-up," Barrow said. "He should be batting every day."

A pitcher does not play every day because he must have rest. So Barrow put Babe in the outfield. That meant Babe could be in the lineup every game.

Other teams wanted to buy Babe Ruth's contract. The Red Sox wanted to keep him. Then the Red Sox owner needed money and sold Babe to the Yankees for $100,000. No club had ever paid that much for a player. That same year Babe hit 54 home runs!

Before that time few players really tried to hit the ball out of the park. They played what is called an "inside" game. They tried for singles and doubles. They bunted and made sacrifice plays in order to help their team score.

But the fans loved to see Babe swat the ball over the fence. He was showing them an exciting new kind of baseball. They jammed the stands whenever he played.

Other batters began to copy the Babe. They began to "swing from the heels," to try and hit home runs. A new, livelier "jackrabbit" ball was being used now

Babe connects for a homer in the 1926 Series.

too. It traveled farther when the bat struck it, and helped pile up homers.

Baseball became a slugger's game. But the Babe was the mightiest slugger of them all. In 1921 he hit 59 home runs, and the Yankees won the American League pennant for the first time.

Babe Ruth was paid $30,000 that year, a huge salary for those days. It seemed especially big to the Babe, who had been so poor as a boy. He had

a good time spending it. He bought a big red car.
He smoked big fat cigars. He gave big parties. He
ate huge meals.

"This is no way to keep in training, Babe!" the
team manager said. "You'll get fat and slow!"

The Babe just laughed. "I can take care of myself," he said.

He spent part of the winter playing exhibition
games. This was against a strict major-league rule.
Babe was in serious trouble.

He was punished for breaking the rule. He was

not allowed to join the Yankees until six weeks after the season started. Even then he was not in playing condition because he had not kept training. His record that year was very poor.

A New York state senator made a speech about the Babe at a baseball writers' dinner. The Babe was there.

"You let our team down, Babe," the senator said. "You let all your fans down. Worst of all, you disappointed all the boys who look up to you as a hero."

There were tears in the Babe's eyes. "You're right," he said quietly. "From now on I will obey the rules. I'll try never to let people down again."

And he did try. But many times after that he broke rules. Each time he was punished in one way or another. Once he paid a $5,000 fine because he refused to obey the team manager. Once he got sick and could not play for weeks, because he ate too many hot dogs.

But when Babe Ruth obeyed the rules, he led his team to the top of the league. His home runs helped the Yankees win the pennant seven times. In 1927 he hit his record of 60 homers.

The Yankees made so much money that in 1923 they built their own stadium. Everybody called the new Yankee Stadium "The House That Ruth Built." On opening day 70,000 fans jammed the stands to watch the Babe. He gave them a good show. He hit a homer with two men on base. The Yankees won the game 4–1.

The Babe always thought he could do anything he wanted. Usually he could. But in 1934 the Babe wanted the Yankees' manager fired. "I don't like him," he said. The owner of the Yankees refused. "If he doesn't go, I go!" Babe Ruth threatened.

Still the owner stood firm. And so Babe Ruth left the Yankees. He joined the Boston Braves the next season. But he was 40 years old. He had been with the majors for 21 years. His great playing days were over. He retired even before the season ended.

He still loved the game. And he still loved children. For the rest of his life he worked to give boys a chance to play baseball. He helped the American Legion organize boys' baseball teams all over the country.

In 1948 Yankee Stadium was 25 years old. Everyone wanted the Babe to attend its big birthday celebration. He was very sick by then. He was soon to die. But he put on his old number 3 uniform once more and walked slowly out onto the field. Thousands of fans cheered. They wanted him to know that they had not forgotten the mighty Bambino.

Fans have not forgotten the Bambino and his home runs to this day. The home run they most often talk about happened in the 1932 World Series.

The Yankees were playing the Chicago Cubs. The Yankees had already won two games. When the Babe trotted out on the field for the third game, the Chicago fans booed him. They wanted to upset him so he would strike out. The Babe laughed.

In the fifth inning the score was tied. Babe had already hit one homer. Now he was coming up to bat again. The fans booed louder than ever.

The umpire called the first pitch a strike. The Babe grinned and held up a finger. He seemed to

Babe's sensational slugging packed the fans into Yankee Stadium in the early 1930s. Here Lou Gehrig greets Babe at the plate after a homer.

be saying, "That's right. It was a strike. So what?"

When the next pitch came over for strike two, the Babe held up two fingers. Now the Chicago fans roared happily.

Then the Babe pointed a finger at a spot in the center-field stands. He seemed to be telling everybody exactly where he was going to hit the next ball.

The pitcher wound up once more. Babe watched him. As always he was holding his head absolutely still. As always his bat was over his shoulder. The end of it twitched just a little, like the tail of a cat about to pounce.

The third pitch streaked toward the plate. The Babe swung and hit. The ball soared high into the air. Every fan lifted his head to follow its flight. The ball disappeared, right into the center-field stands!

For a second there was silence. Then everybody in the ball park stood up and cheered.

It was a gigantic homer. The Yankees won the game. They won the series too.

Later a newspaperman said, "Suppose you'd struck out, Babe, after bragging about where you were going to hit that ball. Wouldn't you have felt foolish?"

The Babe looked surprised. "Gee!" he said. "I never thought of that!"

The Babe was always sure he could do anything he wanted. Sometimes he failed. But not that day in Chicago in 1932. That day he made baseball history.

Lou Gehrig

Iron Man of Baseball

by Willard and Celia Luce

When "Larrupin' Lou" said good-bye to
baseball, he looked back on a record of
2,164 games in seventeen years and a
lifetime average of .340. His was a
fabulous career that ended tragically.

Lou Gehrig
Iron Man of Baseball

The muffled ring of an alarm clock sounded in the dimly lit room. Thirteen-year-old Lou Gehrig reached sleepily under his pillow and turned it off. Then he remembered. He was playing baseball this morning! Lou kicked off the covers and jumped out of bed. He slipped hastily into his clothes.

In the next room Lou's mother and father stirred uneasily in their sleep. Heinrich and Christina Gehrig were proud of their son and worked hard to make a good home for him on New York City's Lower East Side. Two other children had been born to the Gehrigs, but they had died very young. Henry Louis —or Lou, as he was usually called—was their only child now, and all of the Gehrigs' hopes lay in his future.

Lou quickly made his bed, picked up his bat and ball, and tiptoed out the door.

This was the best time of the day to play baseball on the Lower East Side. The families who lived here were poor, and most of the boys had to work after school for a few pennies to help buy food or clothes or pay the family rent. Those boys who loved baseball often had to get up at five o'clock in the morning for a game.

Lou Gehrig was one of these boys. After the ball game there would be school and work and a long evening of study so that someday he could be an engineer. But all he could think about now on this fine spring morning in 1917 was baseball!

Later in the day the city streets would be noisy and crowded. Now the air was cool. There was little traffic, and the streets and alleys echoed hollowly with the crack of the bat, the clatter of racing feet, and the sharp cries of the players.

Whenever two teams decided to play a game, each of the players contributed a penny. With the money collected, they bought a new ball, which was given to the winning team. This was street and sandlot baseball in New York City. Lou Gehrig loved it.

As Lou Gehrig went on through school, he continued playing baseball. He also started playing soccer and football.

When Lou entered high school, he found that he had less and less time for sports. His lessons were more difficult, and he had to study longer hours. He also had to earn more money after school because his father's health was poor. It was not easy for Heinrich Gehrig to find employment. Often he was not well enough to work even when he had a job. He usually worked at iron foundries, where he poured hot, melted iron into molds to make flower designs. This was exacting and exhausting work, and the foundry owners wanted workers who could stand the strain of this heavy labor day after day.

Lou worked in a store. He ran errands and did odd jobs, and each winter he shoveled snow. The small amount he earned from all his jobs helped to keep the family going.

Finally Christina found a job as a cook and house-keeper in a fraternity house at Columbia University. Heinrich took care of the furnace, and Lou waited on tables. Mama Gehrig was the banker of the Gehrig family. She paid the rent, bought the groceries, and somehow kept the family out of debt.

Lou started growing rapidly during the middle of his high school years. Mama Gehrig shook her head. "If he didn't get his meals for waiting on tables, we could never feed him."

"Maybe Louis will be big like a horse," Papa Gehrig suggested. "And strong like a horse too."

"I tell you, it is not a horse we are trying to raise," mama answered. "It's a man, a man with brains."

When Lou finally stopped growing, he was definitely big—he weighed nearly 200 pounds. The fat of his younger years had turned to solid muscle. Soccer was Lou's game now, and he was doing well at it when the high school football coach spotted him.

"Lou," the coach asked, "how come you haven't been out for football? We need big men like you on our team."

"Gosh, I don't know. I'm awfully busy."

"Sure. Sure, I know. But everybody's busy. I'll see you this afternoon on the practice field."

That afternoon Lou was dressed and ready for practice. The coach tried him at tackle and at guard. Lou learned to tackle quickly, and not many ball carriers got past his huge shoulders. Somehow he didn't like playing guard or tackle.

Lou's husky build made him a valuable addition to his high school football team.

One day he said, "Look, coach, I don't like playing on the line."

As he spoke Lou saw the coach's face become red. "Just where would you like to play?" The coach's voice remained low, but Lou could tell he was angry.

"I don't know," Lou admitted. "I think I'd like to carry the ball."

"So you're not good enough just to play. You want to be a hero too. You want to carry the ball! I suppose you want to kick and pass and make all the points." The coach's voice was sharp.

Lou Gehrig shrugged. He understood why the coach was angry. Good linemen were hard to find because everyone wanted to carry the ball and score the points. Nevertheless, playing on the line didn't interest Lou. He said, "If I can't carry the ball, I'll turn in my suit."

"Then you'd better turn it in!" the coach snapped.

Lou did. Before long, however, he was back on the football team, playing fullback. In this position he could kick, pass, and carry the ball. His play was good but not great, although 200 pounds of muscle are hard to stop in any league.

Somehow baseball always seemed to be Lou's real game, and it was here that his great athletic skill began to show itself. He was always a serious player, willing to practice for weeks, months, or even years to improve his playing.

Babe Ruth of the High Schools

Harry Kane was the baseball coach for New York City's High School of Commerce when Lou Gehrig attended the school. Many years later Kane said, "Lou Gehrig was the greatest athelete I ever coached."

During Lou's last year in high school when he was sixteen years old, the school won the Police Athletic League championship.

As a result Lou's team was scheduled to go to Chicago and play Technical High, champion high school team of the Windy City. When Mama Gehrig heard about the trip, she shook her head and said, "No! It is too far for a sixteen-year-old boy to go."

She would not change her mind no matter how hard Lou begged her. Then Coach Harry Kane went to see the Gehrigs at home. "It will be all right, Mrs. Gehrig," he promised her. "Only nine boys are going, and I'll take good care of all of them. They will have good food, get to bed early, and it won't cost Lou a cent."

After some time Christina said, "All right. All right. He can go." She spread her arms to indicate her helplessness. "But you will take good care of Lou?" she pleaded. "He is all the child I have left. Two others have died. I could not stand to lose Louis too."

"Yes, Mrs. Gehrig, I will take good care of all the boys."

The game at Wrigley Field, Chicago, was one of the most important games in Lou Gehrig's baseball career. It put him in the spotlight of the baseball world, and it taught him a great deal about the courage every baseball player must have.

The New York team had only nine players. If one of them got hurt or became sick, Coach Kane had no one to send onto the field in his place.

Al McLaughlin, the catcher, did get hurt. Racing back after a foul ball, he twisted his ankle. The ankle swelled up, and the pain brought perspiration streaming down Al McLaughlin's face. Sometimes Harry Kane had to help him to the plate when Chicago started batting. The coach helped him back to the dugout when Chicago was put out.

Al stuck it out, snagging everything Eli Jacobs hurled from the pitcher's mound.

Eli Jacobs was frightened and sick inside. This was a major-league park where the Chicago Cubs played. The stands were filled with Chicago rooters.

Jacobs lost control of the ball in the first inning, and the Chicago team pushed ahead by four runs. The New Yorkers had no relief pitcher to send in, so Eli went back to the mound, inning after inning. He fought the fear that twisted his stomach into knots. Time after time he drew back and slammed the ball at the plate with everything he had.

Then the New York team started to make a run

here, another there. In the ninth inning, Lou Gehrig came to bat. Two men were out, and the bases were loaded.

Harry Kane put his arm around Lou's shoulders. "Hit it out of the park, Lou!"

Lou Gehrig nodded seriously and stepped up to the plate. The Chicago pitcher drew back his arm, snapped it forward, and the ball streaked across home base.

"Str-i-ike!" the umpire yelled.

Lou Gehrig didn't look at Harry Kane. It had been a strike all right—a fast one right down the alley. Lou shook his head. Then he shook his bat. From one of the bases a New York player yelled, "Sock it, Lou. We want to come home!"

Lou Gehrig clamped his teeth together. He shook his shoulder muscles to loosen them. Then he waited for the next pitch.

The Chicago pitcher flung his arm forward. Again the ball zipped like a silver streak toward the base. Lou Gehrig shifted his body slightly and swung his bat.

The crack of the wood on the horsehide was like a pistol shot. Suddenly there seemed to be no sound at all in Wrigley Field. Every player on the field and in the dugout rose to his feet and stared at the ball. Every fan in the stands leaped up and stood as though frozen.

The baseball shot across the field, clearing the right-field fence, and slammed out of the park.

Suddenly the silent disbelief turned into a roar of applause. These were Chicago fans giving deserved praise to a husky high school youngster from New York. They would long remember Lou Gehrig's grand-slam homer. They would long remember Lou Gehrig.

Newspapers that evening called Lou Gehrig the "Babe Ruth of the High Schools."

Lou Gehrig Becomes a Yankee

Twenty-four universities wanted Lou Gehrig. They wanted him so that he could play football, soccer, and baseball for them.

Finally Lou and his family decided that he should stay in New York and go to Columbia University. He could live at home, and he could keep some of his jobs. Because of his work at the fraternity house, he already knew many of the people associated with the university.

Lou worked hard and did well in his studies. He also made good on the football field and the baseball diamond.

By 1923, however, things were going badly for the Gehrig family. Mama Gehrig became ill with double pneumonia, and papa needed an operation.

One night Lou announced, "I'm going to quit school, mama."

"No, Louis!" Christina cried. "That you must not do!" Tears came to her eyes. "After a little I will be well again, Louis."

"Yes," Lou Gehrig nodded. "After a little you will be well again, but that will not pay for papa's operation. Mama, look . . ." Lou brought his chair close to her bedside. "I can play for the Yankees. They will give me $1,500 now, as a bonus. The bonus is just for signing the contract. Then they will pay me $3,000 for playing next year. It's the best thing to do."

At last Christina Gehrig agreed, and Lou signed with the New York Yankees.

Lou was nearly 20 years old. In addition to weighing some 200 pounds, he stood 6 feet, 1 inch tall. He was a good college player, but he knew that he was not yet good enough to play on a big-league team.

Butterflies fluttered in his stomach that first day in the Yankee locker room. Getting dressed for afternoon practice were many of the great men of the baseball world. Lou had read all about them in the newspapers.

Miller Huggins, manager of the Yankees, shook Lou's hand. "Tell Woodie to give you a uniform, Lou." "Doc" Woods was the Yankee trainer.

Lou got his uniform and a locker, then Woodie said, "Come on and meet some of the boys."

One of the first Lou met was a tall, serious-looking player named Wally Pipp. Wally was the Yankee's first baseman. He was still a great ballplayer, but his hands were slowing a little. His eyes squinted from headaches that often troubled him.

Lou also met Herb Pennock, Waite Hoyt, Joe Bush, and Bob Meusel. Finally there was a big fellow with a great barrel chest, whose tiny, spindly legs looked as though they could hardly carry his huge body. He had a round face and a huge smile. Lou Gehrig couldn't say a thing when Babe Ruth put out his big hand and said in a booming voice, "How are you, kid?"

Playing for the Yankees wasn't exactly as Lou had expected. Every day he reported for practice, and every day he practiced hard. Sometimes he came early; sometimes he stayed late. But during the games he sat in the dugout, wearing out the seat of his pants on the bench.

By August he had been used as a relief first baseman and pinch hitter a total of only thirteen times. His 11 hits gave him 20 bases and an average of .423 —good hitting in anybody's league.

Still, in August, Miller Huggins called him into the office. "Lou," the manager said, "I'm farming you out to the Hartford club in the Eastern League.

Miller Huggins was one of baseball's greatest managers. In later years he became Lou's close friend.

You need more experience than you're getting here. At Hartford you should get to play every day."

As Lou Gehrig left Yankee Stadium that day, he wasn't sure whether to laugh or cry. Leaving the Yankees seemed like failing, and Lou hated to fail. But he loved to play ball, and sitting on the Yankee bench wasn't playing ball.

At first he did poorly with the Hartford team, but soon he hit his stride. He played for them the rest of that season and all the next one.

111

Rookie for the Yankees

The first and second days of June 1925 were important days for Lou Gehrig. He was back with the Yankees now.

On the first of June he went in to pinch-hit for Pee Wee Wanninger, the shortstop. Lou struck out. That game, however, was the first of 2,130 consecutive games in which Lou played. For over fourteen years Lou Gehrig never missed playing in a Yankee game. No one has come close to breaking that record.

On the second day of June, Wally Pipp asked Woodie for several aspirin tablets. Wally's eyes were squinting with pain. Miller Huggins came up as Wally took the pills. "Your head, Wally?" the Yankee manager asked.

The first-sacker nodded. "It's killing me."

"Look," Huggins said, "why not take it easy today? I'll send the kid in and see what he can do."

Wally Pipp looked steadily at Huggins for some time before he nodded. Perhaps he somehow knew that he would never start another game for the New York Yankees. Time had slowed him down, and he knew that a younger man was ready and eager to take his place.

Lou Gehrig was that man. For the next fourteen years Lou held the first-base position against all comers. Even at the beginning Lou was a better hitter than Pipp, but he wasn't as good a baseman. What Lou lacked in experience, however, he made up for in eagerness and ball hustling.

At the plate that first day Lou got a double and two singles against Washington. His batting average shot up. Lou Gehrig's record as a rookie in 1925 was good—better than the team record. He batted at .295 and smashed out 21 home runs, but the Yankees finished only seventh in the American League.

The following year, 1926, was better both for Lou and for the club. Lou boosted his batting average to .313, but only made sixteen homers. That year the Yankees played in the World Series, which went to seven games. The Yankees lost, but Lou did well. His eight hits included two doubles.

The next year, 1927, was a great year for Lou Gehrig and the Yankees. That year Lou captured the record for the most runs batted in, 175. His batting average climbed to .373, and he hammered out 47 home runs. He received the Most Valuable Player of the Year award. The Yankees had the pennant clinched by Labor Day. They won games by scores of 19–2, 12–1, and 21–1. They ended the season with four straight wins over the Pittsburgh Pirates to capture the World Series title.

It was also a great year for Babe Ruth, the Sultan of Swat. That was the year Babe Ruth set his record of 60 home runs in one season. This record remained unbroken until 1961, when Roger Maris slammed out 61 homers.

Although Lou Gehrig and Babe Ruth competed on the diamond, they were good friends. They were the team's leading hitters, and their friendly competition probably helped Babe Ruth set his record.

The batting order worked out by Miller Huggins also helped. One afternoon Huggins watched an opposing pitcher throw four intentional balls and walk Babe Ruth to first base. The crowd booed, but Miller Huggins just stood there hunched over and thinking. The next afternoon he said, "Lou, I want

Lou, off on a hit, shows the strength and grace that made him the "pride of the Yankees."

you to bat right after the Babe today." He turned
to the left fielder, Bob Meusel, "Bob, you'll come
right after Lou."

It didn't take the Yankees long to see the wisdom
of Huggins's new orders. If any pitcher walked Babe
Ruth, Lou Gehrig might smash out a home run and
bring them both in. Should any team have nerve
enough to walk both Babe and Lou, Bob Meusel,
who batted at a comfortable .337, could bring them
both in or at least move them further around the
bases. The batting combination became known as
"Murderer's Row."

That fall some writers claimed that Lou Gehrig,
Babe Ruth, and Bob Meusel won the World Series
before it even started. The Pittsburgh Pirates had
won the National League pennant. The first game
of the World Series was to be played at Pittsburgh.
The day before the series began, the Pirates finished
their practice, showered, and quickly headed for the
grandstand to watch the Yankees work out. What
they saw lowered their morale considerably. During
batting practice the Yankee pitcher threw Babe Ruth
a fast ball. Babe swung gracefully, almost slowly.
The bat caught the ball from slightly underneath,
raising it into a beautiful rainbow arch that ended
over the stadium fence. The Sultan of Swat trotted
easily around the bases and tipped his hat to the
Pittsburgh players sitting in the stands.

Lou Gehrig was up next. Again the Yankee pitcher threw a fast one. This one was right where Lou wanted it to be. Lou swung a fast, powerful, zipping bat at the ball.

One writer described Lou's batting this way, "Lou hit that ball like a Mack truck running into a stone wall at 100 miles an hour." Lou's hit screeched across the field. There was no arch, just a bullet-like ball slowly climbing until it cleared the center-field fence.

The Pittsburgh players looked at one another. No National League player had ever sent the horsehide over the Pirate stadium's center-field fence. Then, almost as though adding insult to injury, Bob Meusel slammed the next ball into the right-field stand. This exhibition put on by the Yankees' Murderer's Row was enough to discourage any team. The New York team won the World Series that year in four straight games.

The Seasons Roll On

The seasons rolled on. Lou practiced hard, and he played hard. The Yankees kept on top, winning more than their share of pennants and world titles.

Lou Gehrig said of the 1928 World Series, "It was one of my greatest." In the third inning of the second game, Lou came to bat. He waited for just the right throw. When it came, he swung with all the power in his massive shoulders and arms. At the crack of the bat against the ball, Lou Gehrig knew he had hit his first World Series home run. As the ball cleared the fence, Gehrig trotted the bases, driving two runs ahead of him.

Encouraged by his base-clearing run, Lou smashed out two more homers in the third game. In the fourth and final game, Lou Gehrig followed up Babe Ruth's four-baser with still another home run.

In the four games, Gehrig went to bat eleven times. He made five runs on six hits. His four home runs tied the record set by Babe Ruth in 1926.

In spite of his fame and records, Lou Gehrig spent considerable time with his parents. He bought a home for them in New Rochelle, a suburb of New York City. Just for the fun of it, Lou gave his mother a present of money every time he made a home run.

Part of Lou's financial success as well as his success in baseball he owed to Miller Huggins, the Yankee manager, who advised him in many ways.

In his spare time Lou went deep-sea fishing with Babe Ruth and Bill Dickey. Dickey was catcher for the Yankees, and for many years he was Lou's roommate when the Yankees were traveling.

During the off season, ballplayers traveled frequently, playing exhibition games. Lou made two trips to Japan and one to Canada. He and his teammates considered these trips fun, for no one worried about winning. The ballplayers were relaxed and enjoyed teasing one another.

The Yankees also had some bad years. During the 1929 season, they went into a slump and could not pull themselves out of it. Then in September Miller Huggins became ill. The Yankee manager was worn out; his face and body had thinned down, and it was only with a great effort that he kept going.

"Hug," the players told him, "you'd better go home and rest. We'll make out."

Huggins shook his head. "I'll be all right," he insisted. Finally the Yankee doctor told him to go to the hospital for a checkup. A few days later Miller Huggins was dead.

His death came as a severe blow to the Yankees and to the baseball world. It was an even greater blow to Gehrig. Miller Huggins had been his close friend, and now the Yankee manager was dead. Without him the Yankees did not play as well as before.

Colonel Jacob Ruppert, a well-known sportsman, owned the New York Yankees. In 1931 when he hired Joe McCarthy to manage the Yankee team, he said, "Joe, I finished third last year. I don't like to finish even second. I like to win."

Joe McCarthy nodded. He knew Ruppert was telling him to win or he wouldn't be manager very long. He said, "I like to win too, Colonel."

"Larrupin' Lou," hands firmly clenched at the end
of the bat, connects for a solid hit.

McCarthy became known as a hard-headed, no-
nonsense manager. Under his leadership the Yankees
once more became accustomed to winning pennants
and world titles.

On the third day of June 1932, the Yankees were
playing the Philadelphia Athletics at Philadelphia.
The warm sun loosened Lou's shoulder muscles as
he waited on deck for his first turn at bat. When it
came, he stepped, almost lazily, up to the plate and
waited for George Earnshaw to throw the ball. When

the ball came, Lou promptly cracked it out of the ball park.

In the fourth inning, Lou collected his second home run. Before the fifth inning ended, Lou Gehrig had made his third home run of the day. When Gehrig stepped up to bat in the seventh inning, Earnshaw had been replaced on the mound by Lee Roy Mahaffey.

As Earnshaw started for the clubhouse, Connie Mack, the Philadelphia manager, motioned him to the dugout. "George," Mack said, "I want you to see how Mahaffey pitches to Gehrig."

On the mound Mahaffey waited for the signal from the catcher. Finally he nodded, wound up, and let go with all the power he had. The ball was fast and high. It was almost at the plate before Lou Gehrig moved. Suddenly the hardwood left his shoulder, streaking outward and around. It crashed solidly into the baseball, sending it out of the field for Lou Gehrig's fourth home run of the game.

In the Philadelphia dugout, George Earnshaw looked at manager Connie Mack. "I believe I see now, Connie," Earnshaw admitted. "He made him hit it to the other field, didn't he?" Mack didn't answer.

A big event took place in Lou Gehrig's life the following year when he married Eleanor Twitchell, a Chicago girl. He had met Eleanor in 1929, but he had not paid her much attention.

He met Eleanor a second time in 1932. She now seemed different from any other girl he had ever met. She was interested in baseball. Eleanor was somewhat quiet and shy so that Lou felt comfortable and easy when he was with her. She was a pretty girl, too, with blue eyes and honey-colored hair. They were married in September 1933.

Babe Ruth Leaves the Yankees

Lou Gehrig was proud of his record of playing in every game, day after day. By the end of the 1933 season, he had played in 1,350 consecutive games, a new record.

Lou almost had to give up the record one afternoon in 1934, but he wasn't known as the Iron Man of Baseball without good reason. He showed up at the ball field as usual, but he was walking with difficulty. His face was twisted with pain.

"What's wrong, Lou?" Joe McCarthy asked.

"It's my back," he answered.

Before McCarthy could tell Lou to take the day off, Lou asked, "I haven't asked for many favors, have I, Joe?"

"No, of course not."

"Then put me first in the batting lineup. Maybe I'll strike out, but that way I can keep my record."

Lou Gehrig did more than strike out. He got a

hit. Somehow he managed to connect with the ball, plopping it into the outfield where it should have been an easy double. With a great effort, Lou reached first base. Here he signaled to Joe McCarthy to send Red Rolfe in to take his place as a runner. By the following day he was feeling better and was able to take his regular place in the lineup. His record was still untouched.

Many times Lou played with injuries that would have benched another player. In 1927 he pulled a muscle in his groin, later he developed more muscle trouble, and then, to top the season off, he sprained his ankle.

Two years later Lou's throwing arm became so sore that he couldn't throw from first base to second. An X-ray showed that he had chipped his elbow, but Lou waited until the end of the season before going to the hospital to have the chip removed.

Three weeks before the 1930 season ended, Lou broke the little finger on his right hand. Instead of reporting it to the club doctor, he bandaged it at home. As a result he had a crooked finger for the rest of his life. In Japan Lou was hit with a fast ball that shattered two bones in his hand, and twice he was hit in the head with balls. In spite of all these injuries, Lou kept right on playing as though nothing had happened to him.

Lou had always played in the shadow of the great

Gehrig catches a high fly to make a putout in a 1936 Yankee-Cleveland game. The great slugger is considered by many to be the number one first baseman in baseball history.

Babe Ruth, the Sultan of Swat. In 1934 Babe retired from the Yankees. With Ruth gone everyone thought that Lou should be the Yankees' big name. Joe McCarthy agreed and made him team captain.

"Why don't you wave and yell up at the stands the way Babe used to do?" some of the players asked Lou.

"Point out where you're going to knock the ball, and then knock it there," others suggested.

Lou Gehrig, however, was Lou Gehrig, and Babe Ruth was Babe Ruth. The Babe, with his big smile, waving arm, and booming voice, was a great crowd pleaser. Lou was friendly and always had a smile, but it was a shy smile, and he always kept himself in the background.

In 1935 Lou slammed out 30 homers and hit .329. The next year was even better for him, but that year the Yankee fans had a new hero to cheer. Young Joe DiMaggio, an outfielder, had joined the team, coming from the San Francisco club.

Tall, dark, and good-looking, Joe was a great ball-player. As a rookie he ran up a hitting average of .329. He crashed out 29 home runs, and he drove in 125 runs. But Lou was still on top, hitting .354 and slugging out 49 homers while driving in 152 runs.

That year, 1936, the Yankees played the New York Giants in the World Series, and Lou Gehrig collected one of his greatest baseball thrills. The great Carl Hubbell was on the mound for the Giants, while Red Rolfe was a base runner for the Yankees. As Lou Gehrig moved toward the batter's box, Joe DiMaggio grinned at him and said, "Over the fence with it, Lou! We need the runs."

Lou stepped up to the plate and waited for the right pitch. Then he blasted the ball into the right-field bleachers. A happy grin covered his face as he chased Red Rolfe across home plate.

Another of Lou's great thrills came the next year in the All-Star game when he faced big Dizzy Dean. Dizzy Dean was then at his peak, retiring player after player with his amazing pitching. Lou lashed out at one of Dean's throws, connected, and sailed the horsehide over the fence for a homer. Once again the familiar shy grin covered Lou's face as he trotted the bases.

Lou Gehrig Benches Himself

In 1935 Lou had continued playing in every game. All through 1936 and 1937, he hadn't missed a game, and he had maintained his batting average above the .300 mark. Then in 1938 his batting average fell below that mark for the first time since his rookie year of 1925.

In spring training the next year, he was still slow. As always he swung hard at the ball, but the horsehide didn't zing away anymore. Instead, it just plopped up and landed in some player's glove, or it barely cleared the infield. Home runs were few and far between.

When fielding, Lou found it hard to get back to first base. Yankee players held up their throws until he was there and ready to catch the ball. Otherwise he missed it, and the runners went for extra bases.

Failing health forced Lou to bench himself after 2,130 consecutive games. He was truly an "iron man."

On May 2 of that year, the Yankees were playing in Detroit. Lou Gehrig told Joe McCarthy, "I won't be playing this afternoon, Joe. I'm benching myself." For a long moment the two men looked into each other's eyes. Finally Joe nodded. "All right, Lou. Maybe if you take a couple of weeks off . . ." Lou shook his head. "This is something more than being tired, or getting old. When you wear out, you don't go all of a sudden like this. You go slowly as Babe Ruth did. This is different. I'm going out to the Mayo Clinic in Rochester, Minnesota. Maybe they can tell me what's wrong."

Lou went to the Mayo Clinic, a great medical center, where he was given a thorough physical examination. The clinic's report read in part:

He is suffering from . . . a form of chronic poliomyelitis—infantile paralysis.

The nature of this trouble makes it such that Mr. Gehrig will be unable to continue his active participation as a baseball player.

Newspaper reporters, ballplayers, and the general public still wanted to know, "But what does it all mean?" Two facts soon became known: Lou Gehrig would not live more than three or four years, and the end would come suddenly and painlessly.

The End of the Road

It was a saddened baseball world that waited for Lou Gehrig Appreciation Day, July 4, 1939. On that day the Yankees were to play two games against the Washington Senators. Between the games the mayor of New York City and others were to make speeches honoring Lou Gehrig. Lou was to make a speech also.

The Yankees had invited all of Lou's ex-teammates, and most of the men were there. While the 1939 Yankee team went out to "murder" the Senators, the older players sat on the benches and tried to outtalk one another.

The big, booming voice of Babe Ruth was missing. Lou Gehrig kept looking around for him, kept listening for the roaring laughter and the powerful voice, but the Babe didn't come.

Lou looked down at the ground and bit his lip. Somehow it just wouldn't be right if the Babe didn't show up. They had been great friends once. During the last years they hadn't been close, but still it wouldn't be right for the Babe not to come.

Then suddenly he was there. A huge smile wreathed his round face. His voice choked a little as he boomed out, "Lou!" The two great ballplayers threw their arms around each other and cried.

When it was time for Lou to make his speech, he

At Yankee Stadium, Lou bid a sad farewell to baseball and his teammates.

stood at the microphone which had been set up at home plate, and looked slowly around him. Sixty thousand people waited.

Many things in life mattered greatly to Lou Gehrig —his wife, his mother, and his father. There was also baseball itself. There were his teammates, the opposing players, the reporters, and the great world of baseball fans.

Lou talked about all these and ended by saying, "I may have been given a bad break, but I have a lot to live for. With all this, I consider myself the luckiest man on the face of the earth."

That autumn Lou received a telephone call from New York City's Mayor LaGuardia. "Lou," LaGuardia said, "I have a job on the New York City Parole Board I wish you would consider."

"I don't know, sir. I haven't had any experience."

"You don't need any experience, Lou. These young fellows have been in prison. They will have to report to you. You've lived a good, clean life, you've been successful, and you should be a good example for them. Just talk to them and encourage them to go straight. Think you can do it?"

"Well, I can surely give it a try, Mr. Mayor."

Lou worked hard at his job on the Parole Board. He was interested in helping those people who had gotten in trouble with the law and now wanted to make a new start in life.

These were busy days, and Lou enjoyed them. But it was evident that his illness was becoming worse. He found it harder to walk, and eventually there were days when he couldn't go to the office. It was the night of June 2, 1941. At first Eleanor thought Lou was just sleeping more soundly than usual. Then she realized that he was actually in a coma. Quickly she called their doctor and Lou's father and mother.

A little after ten o'clock, Lou opened his eyes and looked with a puzzled expression at the faces crowding around his bed. Then, without pain and as though falling asleep again, Lou Gehrig died.

Few men have lived as fine a life as did Lou Gehrig. He came from a poor home, but his family believed in love and respect for one another. He became famous, but fame never went to his head. He made a small fortune, which he spent wisely. And when he knew he was dying, he did not complain, but continued trying to help others.

Lou was elected to the National Baseball Hall of Fame in 1939. His number 4 was retired with him— no other Yankee player would ever again wear that number.

In 1969, at a banquet celebrating baseball's first 100 years, members of the Baseball Writers' Association voted Lou Gehrig the greatest first baseman of all time.

Joe DiMaggio
Yankee Clipper

by Ann Finlayson

The rookie from San Francisco stepped
into the giant-sized shoes of Babe Ruth—
and filled them well. DiMag, as he was
affectionately known, was a powerful
hitter and a talented outfielder, with
a record second to none.

Joe DiMaggio

Yankee Clipper

It was late at night when the phone rang, waking the young ballplayer from slumber. "Who is it?" he inquired sleepily.

The caller was the young man's boss. "I just thought you'd like to hear the news, Joe. You have been bought by the New York Yankees."

Joseph Paul DiMaggio came wide awake. "The Yankees have bought *me*?"

"That's right. Babe Ruth is too old to play another season. They need a new young hitter to step into his shoes. And you're it."

For a moment Joe was too stunned to reply. Then he managed to say, "Well, thanks for telling me. Thanks a lot."

He hung up the receiver and sat back. There would be no more sleep for him that night. He was a Yankee now! What's more, they expected him to be a second Babe Ruth!

As far back as Joe could remember, Babe Ruth had been baseball's biggest star. San Francisco, where Joe lived, was clear across the country from

New York. But San Francisco kids knew all about the Babe.

"Hit it like Babe Ruth!" they yelled at one another in those days. "Make it a home run!"

Joe played third base on the neighborhood team. The other four DiMaggio brothers liked to play ball too. So did just about every boy in the North Beach section of San Francisco.

The neighborhood ball field was a vacant lot. The outfield was all rutted with cart tracks. Rocks marked the bases. Fielders made their own gloves out of padded sugar bags. Sometimes the boys chipped in to buy a ball. But they played a fast, exciting game.

Papa DiMaggio couldn't understand all this excitement about baseball. He was a crab fisherman by trade, working hard to support his nine children. For sport he bowled Italian style.

"I don't like this baseball," he said, shaking his head. "When I need a son to clean my boat, where is he? He's down the street, playing baseball. How can I make fishermen out of lazy baseball players?"

But Joe's mother waved a finger at her husband. "You have your bowling," she scolded. "Let the boys have their baseball."

The two oldest DiMaggio boys, Tom and Mike, became good fishermen like their father. But Vincent, the middle son, got a job in a fruit market and continued playing ball on weekends.

One day Joe's kid brother Dominic came rushing up to him. "Did you hear about Vince?" he cried.

"No, what about him?" Joe wanted to know.

Little Dom was so excited he could hardly stand still. "The Seals have signed him!"

That *was* big news. The San Francisco Seals were one of the best teams in the minor leagues. Many Seal players went right on to the major leagues, which were all in the East and Middle West then.

At supper that night, the two youngsters could hardly take their eyes off their big brother. "Gosh, Vince," Joe said, "maybe you'll be famous someday, like Babe Ruth."

"And what about you, kid?" said the older boy. "It's time *you* started taking baseball seriously."

"Me?"

"You could be good, Joe, if you put your mind to it."

Until then Joe had thought of baseball as a mere game. But Vince's praise set him to wondering. A man could make a career out of baseball if he was good enough. Joe was a modest boy, shy and retiring, but he knew he played good ball.

He joined a Boys' Club team, sponsored by a local businessman. Their sponsor entered them in an industrial league, and they won the championship. Joe played hard.

He was growing into a big, husky youngster with

well-muscled arms. His fielding was a little wild, but he wielded a powerful bat. When he was seventeen, the Seals' scout Spike Hennessy saw him.

"You've got a lot of promise, kid," he said. "You want to work out with the team, so we can look you over?"

"You mean it, Mr. Hennessy?"

"Sure thing, Joe. It's not like being on the team, but you can learn a thing or two watching your big brother."

For a few weeks, the two DiMaggios practiced together. Then came the last three games of the season. The regular shortstop wanted to take off early. Manager Ike Caveney was willing, if they could find someone to replace him. "How about my kid brother?" Vince suggested.

Ike thought it over. Finally he shrugged. "It's too late in the season to hurt us. Get the kid a uniform."

Joe could hardly believe his good fortune. Here he was, actually playing with the Seals!

His first time at bat he hit a triple. Later he got another hit. It was a good showing.

In the field, Joe didn't do so well. He knew he had a powerful throwing arm, and he was afraid of losing control. The first time the ball came his way, he tossed it lightly to the first baseman. It barely got there. "Hey, kid, you throw like a girl!" the other players jeered.

"Well," Joe said to himself, "maybe I'm not as strong as I think."

The next time he got the ball, he threw it with the full force of his arm. It went sizzling past the first baseman into the stand for an error.

The next spring, Joe was invited to the Seals' training school. His throwing arm was still wild, but he had the bat under control. And when the 1933 season opened, the Seals offered him a regular contract. Now there were two DiMaggios in professional baseball.

Young Joe DiMaggio hit safely for the Seals in a record-breaking streak of 61 games.

For the first few days, Joe sat on the bench, await-
ing his chance. Then it came. "Get in there and
pinch hit," Ike Caveney ordered.

Joe took a turn at bat. And when the inning was
over, the manager said, "Go on out and play in the
outfield."

Joe stared in astonishment. "But I've never been
an outfielder!" he protested.

"Believe me, Joe," said Ike, "with that throwing
arm, the outfield is where you belong."

So Joe trotted out to the outfield, and there he
stayed. Ike Caveney was right. Joe's mighty arm
was exactly suited to the outfield. As he matured,
he gained control. Soon he was scooping up line
drives and sending the ball whistling back into the
infield. He caught many an unwary base runner
with his lightning returns.

But batting was still Joe's specialty. He had developed a wide stance and tough, swift wrist action.
When he connected, the ball really traveled. More
than that, you could count on Joe for a hit.

"Have you heard about that kid DiMaggio?" San
Francisco fans began to ask one another. "He hasn't
missed getting a hit in 20 straight games."

"Oh, he's just a rookie, batting over his head,"
some people scoffed.

But Joe's bat showed the skeptics that they were
wrong. Game after game he came to the plate, set

himself with feet apart, cocked his bat, and waited for the pitch. Then, *crack!* another ball went slamming against the outfield wall. Soon his hitting streak reached 30 games.

Now the whole Pacific Coast League was excited. Fans crowded into ball parks to see how long Joe could keep going. "That makes 31 games!"

When the streak got to 40 games, sportswriters started talking about the record. In 1914, the year Joe was born, Jack Ness had hit safely in 49 games. It was a record for the Pacific Coast League.

"Do you think Joe can beat the league record?" fans asked one another.

Joe worked the streak up to 48 games. Then came the game that could tie Jack Ness's record. Joe could not seem to get a hit. In the ninth inning, six men were ahead of him in the batting order. It looked as if the streak were broken.

One teammate slapped young Joe on the shoulder. "The team is behind you, kid. You'll get your chance if we have to break our necks."

Sure enough, all six men managed to get on base. When Joe came to bat, he hit a double.

In the following game, he got another hit, breaking the old record. Then young Joe went blazing on until he had hit safely in 61 games. By then fans all over the country had their eyes on the San Francisco boy. Major-league scouts came running.

Even Papa DiMaggio was impressed. "Maybe this baseball isn't so bad," he admitted cautiously.

For Joe there was only one sad thing about 1933. The Seals decided they didn't need Vince. Joe's big brother went to another Pacific Coast team.

Things looked good for Joe as the 1934 season got started. Big-league teams were looking him over. Even the Yankees were interested. "I'd sure like to play for the Yankees," he confided wistfully to young Dom.

Then in June Joe twisted his knee. He thought nothing of it at first. But soon it hurt so much that he could not play. At season's end, he was still sitting on the Seals' bench.

Baseball scouts shook their heads. Nobody wanted a player with a bad knee. "DiMaggio's just a one-season flash," some reported to their clubs. "Forget him."

Joe tried not to lose hope. But it was hard waiting when everyone was turning away from him.

Then one night came the telephone call from the Seals' president to tell Joe that the Yankees still had faith in him. They had so much faith that they expected him to replace the great Babe Ruth!

First, Joe needed a further year of seasoning with the Seals. Then, in February 1936, Joe DiMaggio went East to report to the Yankees.

The pressure was on, right from the start of spring

training. "So you're the big hitter from the Coast," said reporters. "Do you really think you can take over from the Babe?"

For all the fame that surrounded him, Joe was still shy and tongue-tied. "I can try," he muttered.

Questions came at him from all sides: "Can you hit major-league pitching?"

"Yankee Stadium is a big ball park. Do you think you can cover your share of that outfield?"

"Will you be bothered by those tough New York fans?"

Stories cropped up in the newspapers. "DiMaggio is the greatest rookie since Ty Cobb," some sportswriters proclaimed. Others predicted that Joe would never take Ruth's place. Still others compared him with Lou Gehrig, Tris Speaker, Joe Jackson, and other greats. "DiMaggio," wrote one reporter, "is the Yankees' only hope for the pennant."

It was frightening—the things they expected of him. It was flattering too. But Joe kept his head. "I'm here to do my best," he said simply.

Yes, DiMaggio could hit major-league pitching. He got two singles and a triple in his first game.

Yes, the San Francisco boy could field big Yankee Stadium. In his second game, Joe threw from left field all the way to home plate and pegged the runner out.

No, Joe wasn't bothered by tough New York fans.

In fact, they loved the modest young player. He soon had his own cheering section.

He played so well that in July he was named to the All-Star team. No other rookie had ever been so honored.

All through the summer, the pace kept up. Fans watched Joe. Sportswriters gathered when he appeared.

Babe Ruth had loved excitement and attention. But Joe didn't know how to talk to fans and

Safe at third! Joe hits the bag as a worried third baseman waits for the throw.

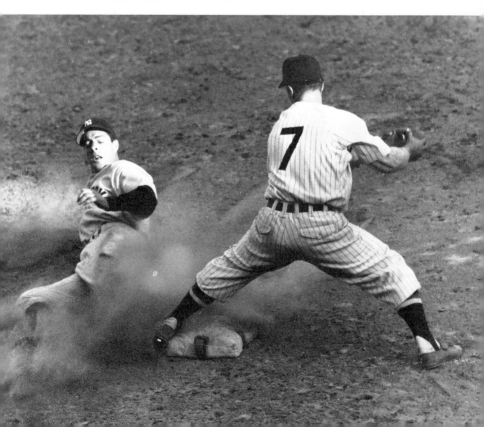

reporters. "Why can't they let me alone?" he often wondered. Like it or not, everything he did was publicized.

The Yankees had not won a pennant in three years. Now, with Joe on the team, they not only won but ended up with a nineteen-game lead. Then they went on to win the World Series.

"Young DiMaggio has given the Yankees new spirit," one writer declared. "Without him, they could never have won."

Joe's hometown agreed. When "the second Babe Ruth" returned to San Francisco, he was met by a brass band. Nobody was prouder of Joe than Papa DiMaggio. "Baseball, that's my sport," he said, hugging Joe.

The pressure eased up a little the next year. But Joe was still the center of attention. Fans were still comparing him to Ruth.

Yankee Stadium's short right-field wall favored left-handed hitters like the Babe. Joe batted right-handed. Nevertheless, he racked up an average of .346 in 1937. And in the seasons that followed, he continued to hit in the three hundreds and twice led his league in batting.

Many experts believed his fielding was even better than his hitting. "He makes impossible catches," said one writer. "But often no one notices it, because he makes fielding look so easy."

"Joe is one of the finest base runners in the game," said another. "He's always trying for that extra base."

Meanwhile, Vince and then Dominic DiMaggio moved up to the major leagues. Vince played for National League teams, but Dom was bought by the Boston Red Sox, one of the Yankees' most powerful opponents.

Then in 1941 history began to repeat itself for Joe. On May 15, in a- game with the Chicago White Sox, Joe got a hit. By itself that was nothing special. But he hit safely in the following game, too, and in the one after that. Soon another hitting streak was on.

Joe didn't like to talk about it. Neither did his teammates. But everyone else did. "Well, Joe DiMaggio has made it 20 straight," people said on the street and in the subways.

"Today's hit makes it 25 in a row for Joe," newspapers reported.

"Here's a bulletin from Yankee Stadium," radio announcers said. "Joe DiMaggio has just hit safely in game number 30."

People began to talk about DiMaggio's setting a major-league record. In 1898, Wee Willie Keeler hit safely in 44 games, the all-time high for the majors. Could Joe do better?

Game followed game, each adding one to his total. Excitement mounted. Yankee fans flocked to the ball park or stuck close to their radios.

Manager Joe McCarthy wanted his star to have every chance. Usually managers give batters instructions on how to hit and what kind of balls to watch out for. But McCarthy decided to let Joe use his own judgment.

On June 21, Joe hit safely in the thirty-fourth game, topping the National League record. Eight days later, he broke George Sisler's American League record of forty-one games. All that remained was Keeler's, set in the days when there was only one major league. On July 1, the Yankees were scheduled to play a doubleheader with the Boston Red Sox.

Joe got two hits in the first game, running his streak to 43. The second game was called at the end of five innings because of rain. But not before Joe had gotten his hit, for 44.

"He's done it!" cried delighted fans. "He's tied Keeler's record!"

"Yes, but can he break it?"

"Tomorrow will tell."

July 2 dawned bright and hot. Joe tried not to be nervous. He called Dom at the Red Sox' hotel and invited him to have dinner after the game. "All right," Dom joked, "but don't expect any favors from me on the field."

In the first inning, Joe hit a long fly to right field, which was taken for the out. His second time at bat

The Yankee Clipper hits safely in his 44th consecutive game to tie Willie Keeler's record!

he caught a beautiful pitch. Back and back it went, toward center field. Joe was sure he had a double —at least. Then at the last minute, the Red Sox fielder made a spectacular catch.

"That was your own brother who caught that!" cried pitcher Lefty Gomez as Joe returned to the bench.

"Yes," he agreed with a rueful grin. "At least it shows that baseball is an honest game."

In the fifth inning, Joe came to bat once more. The crowd was tense and quiet in the 94-degree heat. Veteran sportswriters held their breath. Nine thousand pairs of eyes were on the tall figure at the plate. Joe took his wide stance and waited, bat poised.

Heber Newsome pitched one bad ball, then a second. "Are they going to walk me?" Joe wondered.

But, no, the third pitch was good. Joe fouled it off, and the crowd groaned. Then came the fourth pitch.

Joe swung from his heels. There was a *crack*! The ball went up and out, far over Dom DiMaggio's head. It landed in the left-field stands for a home run.

Keeler's record, which had stood for 43 years, was broken, and by a home run!

The grinning Joe was mobbed as he crossed the plate. "You did it! You did it!" teammates cried.

Lefty Gomez threw an arm around him. "*That's* how to keep Dom's hands off the ball!"

Reporters and radio announcers sent the news out across the nation. "A lot of people have called Joe 'a second Babe Ruth,'" one sportswriter wrote. "But after today, Joe will stand alone."

Joe had a nickname of his own now: the Yankee Clipper.

Joe went on to run his hitting streak to 56 games. He went on to play thirteen seasons of major-league ball. He went on to win three Most Valuable Player awards and two batting championships. He went on to spark the Yankees to ten pennants. And no one expected him to be anything but Joe DiMaggio, the Yankee Clipper.

Often the highest praise showered on Joe DiMaggio has been for his workmanship. He did not make scenes or cause trouble or demand the spotlight. In his quiet way, Joe was all ballplayer, and nobody admired him more than his own teammates.

Joe's last seasons were shortened by injuries and illness. He often kept playing in spite of pain. "If Joe can walk, Joe will play," a friend once said. But at last he was forced to end his playing days.

He put away his Yankee uniform. He returned to San Francisco and went into business. But he never stopped being a baseball hero. Like Babe Ruth's, his name is known to many who have never seen him play.

A few years after Joe left baseball, a reporter was questioning Yankee manager Casey Stengel. "Casey, who's the greatest Yankee of them all?"

Stengel had spent 50 years in baseball. He had seen Gehrig and Ruth. He had managed Mantle and Berra. But after a moment of thought, he answered, "I would have to say DiMaggio. Joe was great doing everything."

Ted Williams
The Boston Kid

by Ann Finlayson

Ted Williams had a reputation for plain talking—and heavy hitting. The Kid rolled up an impressive record that brought the fans in droves to Boston's Fenway Park.

Ted Williams
The Boston Kid

The Red Sox manager took his young outfielder by the arm. "Sit out these last two games, Ted," he urged. "Don't risk your record."

The young outfielder shook his head. "I wouldn't quit now for anything."

It was the last day of the 1941 baseball season. The Athletics were playing a doubleheader against the Boston Red Sox at Shibe Park, Philadelphia. But few people cared about the game itself.

"I came here to see baseball history made," one fan said flatly.

His friend nodded. "I'm a Philadelphia rooter," he said. "But I sure hope the Boston kid makes it."

The Boston kid was Theodore Samuel Williams. He was trying to finish the 1941 baseball season with a .400 batting average.

Since 1887, only eleven major-league players had earned averages higher than .400. Ted's average had been over .400 all season. But in the last few weeks it had slowly slipped down to .399½. Perhaps this season Ted would fail.

"They don't count halves," said one reporter in the press box. "That will go into the books as .400

even. With only two more games left, the kid ought to stay out and play it safe."

A Boston reporter smiled. "Ted never plays things safe. He always gives all he's got."

The first game began with Dick Fowler pitching. Ted came to bat. The first two pitches were balls. Then came the third pitch. Ted swung, and the ball whizzed past the infielders for a single.

Reporters did some quick arithmetic. "That brings him up to .400 even," one said. "Let's see if he can keep it up."

Ted came to bat again in the fourth inning. That time the ball went over the right-center-field wall for a home run.

"That makes it .402," said the reporters. "Come on, Ted baby. Keep going."

For his third trip to the plate, Ted faced a new pitcher, Porter Vaughan. He hit a single.

"That's .403!"

Ted came to bat for the fourth time. The ball traveled over the first baseman's head for another single.

"That makes it .404!"

In his fifth time at bat, Ted got on base through a fielder's error. It did not count.

"Well," said the reporters as the first game ended, "Ted is all set now. He can go without a hit in the next game and still be over .400."

But the Boston man shook his head. "I tell you, this kid is stubborn as a mule. He's never going to stop trying for those base hits."

And so it proved. In the second and last game, Ted came to bat three times. Once he popped out. Once he singled. Once he doubled. Then the game ended.

"Well, that does it!" someone cried. "The kid has hit .406 for the season!"

Some reporters grabbed telephones, while others rushed to their typewriters. Fans poured out of the stands and onto the field. Players, umpires, and officials crowded around Ted.

"Kid," someone cried into the boy's ear, "you're the greatest hitter in baseball!"

Ted grinned from ear to ear. He had wanted to hear those words as far back as he could remember.

Ted had started practicing to be a ballplayer as soon as he was old enough to hold a bat. When he had no baseball, he swung at tennis balls or balls made of rags. He raced to school early so he could play ball before classes started. Little by little, Ted developed a loose and powerful swing.

Ted played on his school teams in junior and senior high school. He also played on an American Legion team and on a team sponsored by a grocery. During his last two years in high school, he batted

.583 and .406. Big-league scouts watched him play and showed interest in signing him up.

At seventeen, Ted Williams was signed to play with the San Diego Padres, a minor-league team. He was a tall, skinny boy. To some he looked too frail to play ball. But others saw greatness in him.

A rival manager watched him bat one day. The manager, Lefty O'Doul, knew something about batting. In his playing days he had twice been batting champion of the National League.

"Don't let them change that swing, kid," Lefty told young Ted. "Stay as sweet as you are."

Ted laughed and promised not to change.

Young Williams had two years with San Diego. Then the Boston Red Sox bought him. They liked his hitting style, but his fielding was awkward.

"You need a little more seasoning, Ted," said Joe Cronin, the Red Sox manager. "We're sending you back to the minor leagues."

Ted's new team was the Minneapolis Millers. When the season opened, Ted went game after game without a hit. He had a quick temper, and his failures made him storm furiously.

"Take it easy, kid," his teammates advised.

But Ted paid no attention. In his anger, he tore up towels and deliberately broke bats. Finally one day he drove his fist at a big glass water jug. The jug smashed. Broken glass cut him across the wrist.

"You're in luck, Ted," the manager said grimly as the gash was bandaged. "You might have been hurt badly."

Ted was ashamed of his tantrum. "I want to make good," he explained. "I want to be the greatest batter in the world."

"Okay, but from now on, do your smashing out there on the field."

The slump soon ended, and Ted's batting became the terror of the minor leagues. But he was still weak in fielding.

His long arms and legs were hard to manage. He couldn't stop and turn easily. Besides, he often forgot all about watching for flies and practiced batting instead.

Once a high fly headed Ted's way. There he stood in left field, glove off, swinging an imaginary bat. "Hey, Ted, wake up!" yelled his teammates.

He came to just in time to make the catch.

But Ted's batting more than made up for his fielding. At the end of the season, he was leading his league, and the Red Sox recalled him.

Ted hit .327 in 1939, his first year with the Red Sox. Babe Ruth said he was the rookie of the year. The second year his average went up to .344.

It took work to keep hitting at that rate. Ted did exercises to build up his arm muscles. He asked for advice from Jimmy Foxx, Bill Dickey, Hank

Ted swung a powerful bat at his first spring practice with the Boston Red Sox.

Greenberg, and other famous hitters. He was out of bed at seven every morning, practicing his swing.

He made a careful study of pitchers, noting each one's special tricks. He knew by heart almost every pitch thrown at him.

"You can only get Williams out when you're new to him," a rival pitcher explained to a reporter. "Once he knows you, you can't fool him anymore."

Ted worked at his fielding too, but he remained awkward for a long time. Many fans thought he wasn't trying. If he missed a ground ball, they booed. If a fly got lost in the sun, they called him names.

Most players pay no attention to razzing. But Ted was sensitive. "I always let them know I'm out there," he said. His quick temper led him into several arguments with Boston fans.

Once he foolishly decided to get back at some rude fans. "I'll strike out deliberately," he decided.

But Ted could not do things halfway even when he wanted to. He tried to foul off the next pitch. Instead, he hit a double.

Reporters liked to tease Ted. Once they followed him on a visit to his uncle, who was a fireman. Ted found the older man sitting contentedly in the sun before the firehouse. "I wish I could take it easy like that," he joked. "Maybe I'll quit baseball and be a fireman."

Reporters wrote seriously, "Ted Williams threatens to quit playing baseball and become a fireman."

Rival teams leaped at the chance to taunt Williams. They blew whistles when he appeared. They yelled, "Fire!" Jimmy Dykes, manager of the Chicago White Sox, handed out firemen's helmets to his players. When Ted came to bat, the White Sox put on the helmets, clanged bells, and imitated sirens.

Ted didn't mind jokes from fellow players. He laughed and went on hitting. Soon rival pitchers became the real victims. "Try pulling a fire alarm!" the Red Sox jeered at them. "Maybe Ted will hop aboard the truck!"

By 1941 there were more cheers than jeers. Ted ended the season with his record batting average of .406. And more than one expert was saying, "Williams is the greatest hitter in baseball!"

The Japanese attack on Pearl Harbor followed close on the heels of Ted's big triumph. Near the end of the 1942 season, he enlisted in the navy as an aviation cadet. In May 1944, he received his wings as a lieutenant in the U. S. Marine Corps. He served as a flight instructor until the end of the war.

Ted's first postwar season was 1946, one of his best. His big day was the All-Star game. He hit one homer early in the game. Then he came to bat again in the eighth inning.

Rip Sewell of the Pirates was pitching for the National League. "Rip has this special pitch. He calls it the 'ephus' ball," Ted was told. "It arches high and comes in slowly. Even when you hit it, it hardly travels out of the infield."

Ted was curious. "I'd like to try one," he answered.

Sewell was willing. His first "ephus" was a called strike. Then he pitched another. Ted took a forward hop, swung, and sent the famed "ephus" ball right out of the ball park.

Rival managers tried many ways of stopping Ted's big bat. Lou Boudreau of Cleveland had the best scheme. Most of Ted's hits were to right field or right center field. Boudreau pulled his fielders over

Home run! Boston's golden boy is safe at home plate.

toward the right. There were no bare spots where Ted could poke a hit, unless he batted toward left field.

"You can hit to left," advisers urged. "Maybe you won't hit the ball so far, but a single is better than nothing."

Stubborn and hot-tempered as usual, Ted answered, "I'm not paid to hit singles."

The Red Sox led the league in 1946. In September they played a game with Cleveland that would clinch the pennant. It was 0–0 in the ninth inning. Then Ted came to bat.

The Cleveland fielders moved over into "the Williams shift." Red Embree pitched. And Ted did what he said he wouldn't do: he hit to left.

"Hey! Look at that ball travel!" screamed Boston fans.

While the Cleveland fielders scrambled for the ball, Ted raced around the bases on his long legs. He had to slide for home, but he made it. It was baseball's most difficult hit, an inside-the-park home run.

That home run won the game, and that game clinched the pennant.

The World Series in 1946 was the only one Ted ever played in. He hit poorly. But he pulled out of the slump in 1947 and won his third batting championship.

Batting still came first with Ted. He practiced constantly and worked hard to keep himself in trim. When he took batting practice, other players stopped what they were doing to watch. They only did that for a master batsman.

Ted's fielding had improved over the years. He seldom missed balls anymore. But some people refused to admit the improvement. "Williams has no team spirit," they complained. "He loafs. He doesn't care whether he catches balls or not."

Ted refused to defend himself against such charges. But his boss backed him up. "He has a big glove out there," said Joe Cronin, meaning that Ted covered a lot of outfield territory. But fans weren't satisfied.

Then in the 1950 All-Star game, Ralph Kiner hit a long fly to left. Ted had to run fast and make a great leap to get his glove on the ball. And as he caught it, his elbow cracked against the wall.

"Did you hurt yourself, Ted?" a teammate asked as they changed sides.

"It's all right. I can finish the game."

Ted stuck it out for eight innings. He made another running catch. He got one hit and popped out twice. But finally he asked to be relieved. They then discovered that he had broken his elbow in that first-inning catch.

"Now nobody can call Ted a lazy fielder," one

reporter said of the incident. "But it's a tough way to have to prove yourself."

Four years later Ted proved again that he had hustle. He was chasing a fly ball in spring practice. He tried too hard, fell, and broke his collarbone.

Ted didn't like people to pry into his private life. He even tried to keep his good deeds secret. When he visited sick children, he always sneaked off quietly.

"That's my business," he replied gruffly when reporters questioned him.

His favorite charity was the Jimmy Fund for children's cancer research. His help brought the fund nearly half a million dollars in contributions.

In 1952 the Marine Corps called Ted back into active service. He was sent to Korea as a jet bomber pilot. He flew 39 missions against the enemy.

One day Captain Williams's plane was badly shot up in action. His radio and other instruments went dead. His brakes wouldn't work, and he couldn't lower the landing gear. His commanding officer signaled him to jump, but he thought he could make it home safely.

As he flew over the landing field, other planes scattered. He brought the plane in on its belly. It skidded and swerved. When at last it lurched to a stop, Ted was surrounded by smoke and flames.

"My gosh, it's on fire!" he cried. He leaped out and ran before the flames could reach the fuel. "If

I'd known it was on fire," he said later, "I'd have listened to my commanding officer."

Ted was 35 years old when he returned to baseball. Most players are retired by then, but Ted still had a lot of baseball in him. He won two more batting championships, beating out young Mickey Mantle. He might have been champion two other years too, but to qualify for the award, a player must have been at bat 400 times. Nervous pitchers had given him too many walks, which did not count as times at bat.

"Think of that!" marveled a rival pitcher. "Williams is 40 years old, and the pitchers are still scared to pitch to him!"

But finally Ted decided that 1960 would have to be his last season.

Ted Williams had made a great record. His lifetime batting average was .344, two points higher than the great Babe Ruth's. He belonged to that tiny group of men who have hit over .400. He won six American League batting championships. Four times he led the league in home runs. Twice he won baseball's Triple Crown, ranking first in batting average, home runs, and runs batted in. Five times he was voted the league's Most Valuable Player. And, proving that he had intelligence as well as skill, in 1969 he was brought out of retirement to manage the Washington Senators.

"Williams lost five years to the Marine Corps," experts point out. "He suffered a lot of bad injuries. Pitchers gave him all those walks. Think what records he might have set if he'd had better breaks!"

Ted came to bat for the last time in Fenway Park, Boston. It was exactly nineteen years to the day since that doubleheader in Shibe Park. And he was still giving all he had.

His first time at bat, pitcher Jack Fisher of Baltimore walked him. He popped out the second and third times he was up. Then in the eighth inning, Ted Williams came to bat for the last time in his playing career.

Fisher wound up and threw. Ted swung—the same loose, beautiful swing he had developed on the San Diego playgrounds long ago. And the ball went out of the park.

Index